Image Guidance
and Healing

Elizabeth-Anne Vanek

PAULIST PRESS
New York/Mahwah, N.J.

Library of Congress Cataloging-in-Publication Data

Vanek, Elizabeth-Anne, 1951–
    Image guidance and healing / Elizabeth-Anne Vanek.
        p.   cm.
    ISBN 0-8091-3508-6 (paper)
    1. Imagery (Psychology)—Therapeutic use—Case studies.
    2. Visualization—Therapeutic use—Case studies.   3. Mental
    healing—Case studies.   I. Title.
    RZ401.V34   1994
    616.89′14—dc20   94-16221
                                                                CIP

Published by Paulist Press
997 Macarthur Boulevard
Mahwah, NJ 07430

Printed and bound in the
United States of America

Contents

For Elizabeth Ann Houlihan
whose courage, determination and zest for life
have been an inspiration

Introduction

When I had finished transcribing the last case study for *Image Guidance: A Tool for Spiritual Direction* (New Jersey: Paulist Press, 1992), I thought I had written the final word. Yes, there would be new clients to work with and new stories to tell, but I believed they would fall into the categories I had established in my book and that they would simply illustrate "more of the same." As usual, I had underestimated the power of the unconscious. Time and time again, I have been surprised into new awareness and new possibilities. When things have seemed most settled and most satisfactory, the unconscious has called me—subtly at times, vociferously at others—to new adventures. And I have heard the call and responded.

As I explained in *Image Guidance: A Tool for Spiritual Direction,* the process of using the active imagination in counseling contexts came to me "from nowhere." I do not have a background in psychology, nor had I, at the time, explored much in the way of Jungian thought, beyond dream analysis. In fact, most of the reading I have now done on the subject was for the purpose of revising the manuscript of *Image Guidance:* I first wrote the book, then incorporated supporting data. Where my own insights had come from was lived experience; these stories I relate in my earlier book and so I will not go into them here. It is enough to point out that the process I have named "image guidance" broke into my life in various dramatic ways. Moreover, it is the clients I have worked with who have taken image guidance forward through their own unique circumstances, insights and needs.

I see myself primarily as a vehicle of the unconscious, using a tool which has been presented to me for the good of many. Along the way, clients have learned to use it during sessions in which they themselves function as guides. I do not regard image guidance as my property or invention—it is, after all, a very human activity which does not only belong within the context of spiritual direction; however, I do caution all those who use it to recognize the power of this process and to treat it with respect: in the wrong hands or used in the wrong situations, the active imagination *can* be dangerous.

In this new book, I continue to explore some health applications of the image guidance process. I began this exploration in *Image Guidance: A Tool for Spiritual Direction,* but have taken this work to new depths. What began as a limited exploration of how image guidance could help a client with diabetes has expanded into applications as varied as dealing with food addictions, preparing for childbirth, learning from cancer and coping with paralysis. Much of the encouragement to pursue new health applications came via Judith-Rae Ross, my diabetic subject. Her medical caregivers had been impressed by the improvements they noted in her condition—improvements which she herself attributed to our working together. It was their feedback which led Judith and me to discuss the possibilities of collaborating on a workshop for nurses to be held at DePaul University, where we both teach. Our main focus was to be the explorations we had undertaken together, but to supplement our data, each of us looked for new subjects who would be willing to face their illnesses, disabilities or addictions through image work while continuing with traditional medical interventions. The results of these findings I present in this book.

Elizabeth-Anne Vanek

Image Guidance: The Process

"Image guidance" is the name I have coined for the very ordinary activity of observing one's own spontaneous images, for dialoguing with them and allowing them to provide guidance. Anyone who has ever indulged in daydreaming or who has allowed images from waking or dreaming to flit before one's eyes like images on a movie screen is familiar with what Jung called "the active imagination." Jungian analysts regard the active imagination as the most powerful tool for exploring the unconscious. Robert Johnson describes the power that is released when we consciously take part in the drama of our imaginations: "the ego actually goes into the inner world, walks, talks, confronts and argues, makes friends and fights with the persons it finds there. . . . Although it is a symbolic experience, it is still a real experience involving real feelings" (*Inner Work,* 140–141). At the same time, many Jungians see active imagination as a solitary task; for example, Barbara Hannah, a student of Jung's, defines the active imagination as "a very individual and even lonely undertaking. . . . I could never do active imagination with anyone else in the room, however well I knew the person" (*Encounters with the Soul: Active Imagination,* 12). It is because image guidance provides a method for using the image making faculty within counseling contexts, under the direction of a guide, that it goes beyond what is usually meant by "active imagination." Though my own context for using image guidance is generally spiritual direction, I define "guide" as anyone who facilitates another's encounter with truth-revealing images.

Image guidance is not an end in itself, but a valuable tool for connecting with buried issues, for clarifying complex situations, for understanding emotions, for discovering the source of dis-ease (whether spiritual or physical), and for tapping into the inner wisdom that exists within all of us. When people come to see me, I don't automatically assume that I will use image guidance with them. My first concern is to listen to their stories, to ascertain *what* they are looking for, and to consider how I can best be of help. This is particularly true in spiritual direction where the primary concern is relationship with God; using image guidance may or may not help deepen this relationship and so I must pay attention at all times to the needs of the particular directee. When someone comes to me specifically to work with images, I may find myself doing more listening than image work for much of the session, and if an ongoing working relationship develops, there may be sessions where we do not work with images at all. Whether the context is spiritual direction or some other form of active listening, what is important is that I—or whoever else happens to be guide—have the flexibility to move between different ways of being present to the client. And this, of course, takes intuitive skills. Ideally, the guide is someone who is well-practiced in counseling skills, whether as a pastoral counselor, a therapist, a chaplain, a bereavement counselor or in any other role which requires empathy and discernment. A thorough grounding in myth and symbols and a sensitivity to poetic expression are also invaluable.

Also crucial is the ability to discern who is a potential candidate for image guidance and who might not be ready for the process. Barbara Hannah cautions that "misunderstood and indulged in, rather than regarded as a scientific piece of hard work, it (the active imagination) can release forces in the unconscious that can overcome us" (6). Anyone who has suffered from a recent trauma, anyone whose ego boundaries seem thin, anyone whose emotions are raw may be too vulnerable for the process. Screening tools (see pgs. 132–34) are useful devices for evaluating when and when not to use image guidance. For the most part, however, intuition and common sense are the best guides. I have had clients with whom I have agreed to meet on the condition that they are simultaneously in therapy and clients whom I have referred to therapists as a result of our work together. There are also those for whom image guidance has never been an option because I have been concerned about dangerous outcomes. I think particularly of one college student who suffers from chronic depression and whose grip on reality seems tentative at best.

The basic stages of image guidance are as follows:

1. allowing the image to surface
2. examining the context from which the image arises
3. emptying oneself through deep breathing and relaxation
4. encountering the image with the assistance of verbal directions given by the guide
5. dialoguing with the image while sharing with the guide what one has seen and felt
6. returning to "ordinary" consciousness
7. processing the experience with the guide

How much time is spent on each of these stages depends on the client's needs and on my own assessment of what is appropriate. It may take a few minutes to surface an image or half an hour of exploration. Extensive breathing exercises may be necessary to relax the client or simply the instruction, "close your eyes and focus on the image. . . ." The three-way conversation between client-image-guide may take five or ten minutes or as long as an hour. Similarly, the return to waking consciousness may be the abrupt instruction, "when you are ready, open your eyes," or there may be a long process of offering comfort, suggesting options, having the client express gratitude to the image or having him or her repeat self-affirmations. In some form or another, however, each of these stages is present during the process. The other constants include: the use of a dimly lit quiet room where there will be no interruptions; a comfortable setting (I sometimes invite clients to lie down on the couch); the assurance that we can stop the process at any point where it becomes too uncomfortable for the client. In the next chapter, I provide some suggestions on how to use image guidance without a guide.

Though this book is primarily about the health care applications of image guidance, I need to stress once again that I am neither a psychologist nor a medical practitioner. I do, however, consider myself to be a healer of the spirit, and in my work as spiritual director I *do* come across people in need of physical healing. In reading the works of medical doctors who use imagery techniques as part of their healing regimen, I feel affirmed in my use of image guidance for health purposes. Jeanne Achterberg, author of *Imagery in Healing: Shamanism and Modern Medicine,* writes:

> . . . healing with the gifts of the imagination, long the province of the shaman, has taken on an extraordinary new direction. No longer are these talents considered the exclusive territory of a privileged few; now they are accessible to all as a function of developments in medical practice. The common element in each of the techniques discussed . . . is the

active participation of the patient. In the modern
health setting, the healee also becomes the healer,
while the shaman dons the role of teacher (111).

Perhaps in using image guidance for purposes of physical healing, I am adopting the role of shaman while allowing
the client to find the resources for his or her own healing
within the self. By encouraging clients to dialogue with their
own spontaneous images, by inducing altered states of consciousness, the guide sets the stage for self-healing; conventional intervention may still be called for—and, in fact,
should not be terminated without the full approval of medical caregivers—but the client becomes an active participant
in the healing process and is more fully in control of the
outcome.

In her book, Achterberg explains how imagery can pro-
duce physiological changes in patients, relieving not only
stress and fear, but also identifiable symptoms. Bernie Siegel, who like Achterberg demonstrates that "body and mind
are different expressions of the same information," quotes
Pert and Ruff, researchers of the physiological basis to the
unconscious:

> For Freud and Jung, the unconscious was still a
> hypothetical construct. For us, the unconscious
> more definitely means psycho-biological levels of
> functioning below consciousness. Deep, deep un-
> conscious processes are expressed at all physiologi-
> cal levels, down to individual organs such as the
> heart, lungs, or pancreas. Our work is demonstrat-
> ing that all the cells of the nervous system and endo-
> crine system are functionally integrated by net-
> works of peptides and their receptors (*Peace, Love
> and Healing*, 36–37).

Siegel himself states that "we may be able to change what takes place in our bodies by changing our state of mind. Therefore, when we experience mind-altering processes—for example, meditation, hypnosis, visualization, psychotherapy, love and peace of mind—we open ourselves to the possibility of change and healing" (21).

All this has practical implications. Through mental rehearsals of painful or dangerous procedures, clients can condition themselves (or "psyche themselves up") to react the most favorably during the actual events. Moreover, by assessing their clients' images, health care practitioners not only can diagnose conditions and clients' attitudes toward their physical state, but can also implement image therapy which is specifically related to each individual case. These health care applications for imagery lie beyond my expertise and rightly belong in a clinical setting, but they do illustrate the optimum situation of the healer who is both shaman and scientist:

> . . . those who heal in the imaginary realms must also understand and speak the language of the scientist in order to establish credibility and be embraced within the medical community. The finest medicine will be practiced by those who take the best from the shaman and the scientist (Achterberg, 75).

In both my books on image guidance, my main concern is to present the client's experience and to insert analytical comments along the way. However, what "happens" to the guide is also important. I have found that by participating in the imaginative experiences of the client, I am both objective guide and subjective participant. Even as I analyze the images which unfold before me, even as I observe the client's facial expressions and body language, even as I remember the context out of which the images developed, my emotions are highly involved in the client's narrative. I see what the client sees, I hear what the client hears, I feel what the client feels, but at the same time my professional self is at work, making connections, intuiting meaning, evaluating, facilitating, and making decisions about closure.

In one workshop I gave—to a team of psychologists—the degree of empathy I experienced with my subject was striking. Though we were working together in a public context—which is almost impossible with an essentially private process like image guidance—I experienced an emotional "bonding" with the client which was so intense that I entered into his pain as well as into the images. As he described the ramparts that had been constructed around his heart, as he described the incredible effort involved in holding "enemies" at bay, I suffered with him. In my desire to liberate him from his need to keep others out, I found myself moving more and more deeply into his experience. I forgot audience, I forgot the fact that I was offering a professional in-service, and allowed myself to be vulnerable.

Focusing on the image of his constricted heart, I asked Francis if there was anyone who could help him break down the ramparts.

"I can see a soldier or two," he said. "Perhaps there are three or four of them. There's not much *they* can do."

"Ask them if they would be willing to work as a team," I instructed. "See if their collective efforts could make a difference."

"They said yes," said Francis. "They've grouped together and they're making an assault on the walls. They rush at the heart and the ramparts topple—I feel as though a steel band has snapped inside me. My heart can beat again, can feel again . . . something very powerful has happened. . . ."

My own eyes were closed—something I rarely do, as I like to monitor the client's responses. Intuitively, I knew Francis was crying; I felt tears form in my own eyes.

"Thank the soldiers for helping you," I said. "Notice how your heart is expanding, how much room there is for everyone within your heart. Look at all the people you can now let in, all those people who so very much long to be part of your life. Feel how much they care about you; feel how good it is to accept their friendship. Spend some time with them, enjoying their company. Then, when you are ready, open your eyes."

As we processed the experience, it was clear that my felt empathy had allowed Francis the safety to enter his images without any fear of being judged. For my part, the engagement of my own emotions in the subject's symbolic narrative had heightened my sensitivity to his needs; this, in turn, sharpened the intuition upon which I depend for so many of my responses. I was able to guide from the heart. The subject was empowered to put new energy into several previously painful relationships; I felt touched by that power and left the workshop feeling both energized and moved. This experience of sharing in the subject's suffering is becoming a significant factor in my work as healer. Though there are varying degrees to which I become emotionally involved in an image guidance session, the compassion that this generates encourages the client to let down defenses and to participate fully in the therapeutic process. The "down side" of this is that there are occasions when I feel the clients' pain, know what they need to do, and yet am forced to realize that any power to effect change comes from within them, and not from me. I remember, in particular, working with someone who seemed to be mildly depressed whenever I met with him. He visualized his depression as a chain and ball attached firmly to his right leg; when I suggested that he could try to remove the chain, he followed my instructions (visually speaking, that is), but continued to drag his leg. For him, the prospect of being liberated from depression was more frightening than the ball and chain which so effectively limited him. He preferred to remain as he was, rather than to embark on a journey of change. I still remember how profoundly sad I felt as the session came to a close without bringing a happy resolution for either of us.

The experience of awe in the face of mystery is another way in which I, as guide, have been affected. Though I use image guidance as one of many tools in spiritual direction, I also use it in counseling contexts which are not specifically religious. What has amazed me is that while I may take care to avoid imposing my own beliefs or symbols upon clients, invariably the encounter with personal images does involve a "religious" dimension. Clients who claim to be atheists, agnostics and cynics have encountered hooded monks, the stereotypical image of God as Father, and a wide range of wisdom figures; those who may be seeking my services for spiritual reasons frequently encounter religious symbols from within their own traditions. In each case, these symbols arise spontaneously from the unconscious, bearing messages about achieving wholeness of body and spirit, about making life-giving choices, and about becoming spiritually grounded. As I listen to the client report what he or she has seen and heard, I not only observe physical and emotional reactions, but also undergo shifts of my own. At times, an encounter with religious symbols becomes a holy moment in which both client and guide are conscious of the presence of otherness in the room.

As a consequence of my work in imagery, I have not only companioned others in their inner work, but have also entered more deeply into my own center of self. My work in helping others to find wholeness has brought me into the territory of pain and into the sacred ground of mystery;

touched by both, I find myself receiving the gifts of compassion and wonder—two gifts which are indispensable for anyone who is authentically committed to the art of healing.

As a healer without medical training, I can use image guidance to explore the psycho-spiritual roots of physical problems, to foster a harmonious relationship between disease and sufferer, to examine a client's attitudes and options, to relieve stress, and to help the client learn from his or her illness or disability. More physiologically-based image work—i.e. work that involves detailed knowledge of how the body functions—I leave to those who are more qualified.

Image Guidance without a Guide

Even without a guide, we can allow images to lead us into mystery and into all the revelations to be found there. The image is a gift to help us grow, and what it means is something we already know deep within ourselves, even if our conscious minds have not yet grasped the meaning. These are helpful steps to follow when using image guidance for purposes of healing:

1) Be aware of the condition about which you need some clarity. Reflect on your symptoms and about the impact they have had on your day to day life.

2) Be clear about your expectations of the imagery process. If you are looking for complete remission of symptoms, then you will probably be disappointed. Focus, instead, on more possible outcomes: new understanding as to why you may have become ill or disabled at this time; a deeper sense of acceptance; an awareness as to what you can learn from your illness or disability; insights about possible lifestyle changes which could help you to live more fully; a sense of other possible interventions which might ease your condition. . . .

3) Ask yourself if you are really open to healing, in whatever form healing takes. Some people cling to their symptoms because they have become accustomed to them, and this interferes with the success of the image guidance process.

4) See what images come to mind that reflect your physical condition; when one "fits," spend some time focusing on it—draw it, if possible.

5) When you feel really in touch with your image, relax yourself through breathing techniques. Empty your mind of everything except your image. Tune out all background noises and distractions.

6) Become the spectator; watch your image unfold without analyzing it or judging it. Be aware of how you are feeling as it moves through different stages.

7) Interact with your image. Ask your image any questions you may have concerning your health. Listen for its answers and ask new questions, as appropriate. Go as deeply as possible. When one question yields nothing, rephrase the question or ask something else. Don't be surprised if it seems to be your own voice that is answering you. Trust the answers that come, provided that they call you to life.

8) When you feel that the image has yielded its wisdom to you, thank it for what you have learned. If you are comfortable with this, spend some time in prayer, conscious of new awareness.

9) Upon your "return," reflect on what the experience has meant to you. Journal about new insights.

10) Test your new insights with your health caregivers. Do not make any changes involving medication, physical or psychological therapy, or medical procedures without careful consultation.

Image Guidance:
Some Health Care Applications

1) To help the client focus on his or her physical condition so that the health care practitioner can authorize appropriate diagnostic tests.

2) To help the client transcend fear and pain and to cooperate with his or her caregivers.

3) To help the client acknowledge shock, fear, anger or disbelief and to understand these reactions more fully.

4) To assist the client in adjusting to loss (e.g. loss of speech or vision, loss of a limb, loss of reproductive faculties, loss of a baby, loss of mental abilities, loss of looks, etc.).

5) To help the client to move beyond trauma and into a future that is as productive as possible.

6) To assist the client in fighting pain.

7) To enable the client to confront approaching death.

8) To assist the client to become an active participant in the recovery process.

9) To encourage the client to see the spiritual dimensions of his or her situation.

10) To empower the client to live in harmony with any chronic or irreversible situations.

Image Guidance and Accidents/ Rehabilitation

Accidents interrupt the flow of life, catching people off guard, often leaving devastation behind them. Without any warning, an ordinary day at work or a simple excursion can end in disaster—a fall down the stairs, for example, or an entanglement with machinery, or the collapse of a parking garage. The possibilities for such disasters are endless: I think of a friend whose eyes were burned when a hot tea bag exploded in his face; I think of the time the overhead garage door swung down while I was backing out of the garage, destroying the rear of my van; I think of only yesterday when my sixteen year old son, on his way to school, rammed into another car, totaling both so effectively that it is a miracle that any of the seven people involved walked out alive. What is so terrifying about accidents is that they strike at random: there is no way of immunizing oneself against them. While being "centered" and alert can sometimes spare one some of the time, no one can claim to be accident-free. To be human is to experience the arbitrariness of life, and accidents are part of this arbitrariness.

When an accident leaves disabilities in its wake, the process of image guidance can be a useful tool for helping those affected to come to terms with what has happened to them.

Questions of "Why me?" and feelings of guilt and anger have spiritual ramifications which need to be addressed; moreover, facing a future of seeming diminishment in terms of one's functioning or appearance can be overwhelming. Here again, image guidance can help clients to confront their own feelings and issues, and to discover "Where is God in all of this?" If the accident results in death, then sometimes dialoguing with the deceased through the imagery process can bring a sense of peace and resolution which would otherwise be impossible. If the accident was caused by another's negligence, then the issue of anger can be faced. If the subject was responsible for the accident, then feelings of guilt can be explored. Through image guidance, it is possible to regain hope in a very real way, even if the subject feels himself or herself to be in a seemingly hopeless predicament.

Before proceeding with imaging an accident, it is important to discuss the causes and consequences of the accident, together with the client's feelings. It is also important to discover what the client hopes to achieve through image guidance. Obviously, no amount of imagery is going to undo the fact that an accident did occur and that it has consequences; however, if the client hopes to achieve greater peace of mind, to find hope in the midst of darkness and to envision a future of possibilities, then image guidance might be a useful tool. As always, the guide needs to discern whether the seeker is emotionally ready to face his or her situation. The more recent the accident, the more the seeker and guide need to proceed with caution: it takes time for accident victims to reach a place of acceptance, and time for them to realize the full implications of what has happened to them and to others who may have been involved.

If the guide determines that the seeker is indeed ready to face all the implications of the accident, then the initial session should include the following questions:

1. What do you see?
2. Does the accident have a form?
3. Does the accident want to tell you something?
4. Is there something you see now that you didn't see then?
5. Is there something you are learning?

Just as in working with a disease, so in working with an accident, the accident can become integrated with the self and can be a source of revelation. The client may find that the accident and its aftermath can be sources of inner growth with lifelong benefits. What may have initially seemed like a tragedy and a dramatic interruption of life may, in fact, ultimately be "useful."

The process of rehabilitation is, in part, a process of rediscovery. Through openness to this process, the client will not only learn coping strategies, but will also discover his or her new self since the accident, and will be able to draw strength from these insights. Shifting attitudes, shifting values and shifting relationships may all be part of this experience; in fact, if nothing changes, then it is probable that the client is in complete denial about what has occurred. The emphasis of imagery during this process can be for the client to come to terms with the injury, with the self that has developed since the accident and with the new way of life that accompanies it. Concerns that surface during image guidance can be shared with the client's health care professionals.

While each image guidance session needs to be tailor-made to the individual client, there are some questions which the guide needs to introduce along the way:

1. How does the client image the injury?
2. Can the client speak to the injury and/or the injury speak to the client?
3. What does the injury want the client to know about its

nature? What does the client want the injury to know about his/her nature?

4. How does the injury feel? How can the pain be eased?

5. How is the treatment affecting the injury? What does the injury want the client to know about the treatment? What does the client want the injury to know about the treatment?

6. If the client cannot take full advantage of the treatment or of the prescribed regime, why? What does the injury want from the treatment? What suggestions does the injury have for more effective treatment?

7. Can the client embrace the injury? If the client is able to do this, he/she should be asked how this felt. If the client cannot embrace the injury, then the reasons for the distance should be discussed.

8. How does the client image himself/herself since the accident? How does this image differ from the former self?

9. Can the client speak to the new self? Can the new self speak to the client?

10. What does the client want the new self to know? What does the new self want the client to know? How can they learn from each other?

11. What does the client love, like or admire about the new self?

12. What does the client wish were different about the new self?

13. How can the new self measure up the client's expectations?

14. How can the client accommodate himself/herself to the new self?

15. Can the client embrace the new self? If not, the reasons should be pinpointed and later discussed.

16. What does the injury have to say to the new self? What does the new self have to say to the injury? What does

the client have to say to both of them? Any animosity between the injury and the new self should be explored.

17. How can the injury and the new self benefit more from the prescribed treatment?

18. How can the client, new self and injury live together in the most advantageous way? What has the client learned from the injury? What are the positive aspects of the future and the new way of life since the accident/injury? How can the client come to peace with the injury and the new self?

As with any application of image guidance, the benefits derived will depend on the client's willingness to grow, trust in the guide, and on his or her surrender to God, or whatever that person names as relationship with ultimate reality. The following case study presents the way I worked with one particular client over the course of a year. I simply present what happened during the sessions, with little analysis along the way. Through the transcriptions of the various sessions, readers will observe how the client moved from cynicism and spiritual atrophy to hope, self-acceptance and a deep spiritual grounding. Some of the images reoccur over and over again, while others spring up, seemingly from nowhere. Many of the themes repeat themselves in a variety of forms, always prompting the seeker to move toward integration.

When Elizabeth first wheeled herself into my office, it was in response to a letter I had sent disabled students on campus. I was looking for subjects to help me in my development of new applications for image guidance, and Elizabeth happened to be one of those who responded. I knew nothing about her beyond the fact that she had been paralyzed in a car accident three years earlier; for her part, she knew only what my letter had outlined about the process we would be using. She seemed enthusiastic about the work we would be doing, but also a little nervous. During our initial conversation, I tried to ascertain whether or not she would be a good candidate for image guidance. My main concern was that emotional backlash from the accident would make the process too painful for her; as she spoke about her paralysis, I not only listened to the "facts" but also tried to observe her reactions. Any future work we did together would be influenced by my full understanding of her situation and of her general attitude toward it.

Without any display of pain or self-pity, Elizabeth described the eventful winter night three years before when she and a group of friends had hit a patch of ice and skidded across an expressway, into an oncoming semi-trailer. Asleep on the back seat, she had been the most severely injured and was, in fact, lucky to have survived. A long hospital stay, followed by repeated back surgeries, made it necessary for her to transfer schools and move back home. As I listened to her story, I found myself picking up different emotions from those I expected. Instead of anger or grief, I was hearing frustration and boredom. There was no sense of "Why me?" or any expressed fear about the future. What I heard was that Elizabeth missed her friends from her previous school and her independence; in addition, she was bored with her present courses and was impatient to graduate so that she could work in her chosen field, sociology. I heard no complaints about limitations or even about more major surgery; rather, I heard irritation about the "time setback" another prolonged hospital stay would entail.

I was not only struck by the issues she identified, but also by my own reactions to her. Her feisty attitude made it difficult for me to see her as "disabled"; in fact, Elizabeth said that her friends often forgot she was in a wheelchair and would sometimes say "Get it yourself!" when she asked them to pass her a book or anything else that was not within easy reach. Though of slight build, she had a strong presence and I quickly felt she could do anything with her life that she wanted. From her comments about boredom and from her general articulateness, I also sensed that she was bright and possibly cynical.

Elizabeth had brought no images with her but she was curious about a recurrent dream she had four times on the night of her accident, while she was in intensive care. It had been a frightening dream and she often wondered what it had meant. In it, she was a child playing in a playground; then, in the next sequence, she saw herself in a derelict house, holding a tool box. From there, the dream shifted to a terrifying pursuit in which a man chased her to a garage; in all four dreams, she would run to her car, turn on the engine and see everything explode around her. Then, in the final sequence, she would see herself plunging into a deep body of water, gasping for life.

Water, it turned out, was something she feared. We agreed to re-enter the dream, using image guidance. Even though our earlier conversation seemed to indicate that Elizabeth had already "processed" the accident and its implications, I was concerned that the experience would surface forgotten pain or pain that had been repressed. I led her through breathing exercises, inviting her to imagine that she was protected by a white light and that she was accompanied by a close friend. I also emphasized that we could stop the process at any time, if she felt uncomfortable.

Once back in the dream, Elizabeth found that everything had become sketchy; the framework of her dream existed, but nothing more. There was the playground fence, but no playground equipment or children; there was the frame of the house but nothing more; even the garage and the car had become shells of themselves. I asked her to confront the stranger who was pursuing her and to ask him what he wanted, but he disappeared. I instructed her to get in the car and refuse to turn on the engine, but there was no car in sight. All that was real was the water.

"I know that you are afraid of water, Elizabeth, but it might be helpful to focus on the water. None of the images seems to have much significance anymore. If you feel comfortable doing this, describe what you can see."

"It's a vast expanse of water, but it's blue and bubbly, not like the dark water in the dream. I don't feel quite so afraid of it."

"Focus on the water, Elizabeth. In your dream, you saw yourself almost drowning. Can you tell me what is happening now?"

"Well, I'm back in the water, going down, deeper and deeper, but it is beautiful and safe. I feel peaceful—almost as if I belong in the water. And the deeper I go, the more at peace I feel."

"So the sense of threat has gone?"

"Yes."

"What else has changed?"

"I no longer feel pursued—it's as though things have fallen into place. I feel as though I'm where I'm meant to be."

When we processed the session together, several things were apparent. In the first place, whatever purpose the dream had initially served seemed largely irrelevant. If the dream had come to help Elizabeth face the crisis or to provide an emotional release for her, it had done its job. The time of the playground, the time of childhood, was over; the time of building and of controlling construction had shifted. Things had exploded, had shattered, but Elizabeth had learned to live with the pieces and to rearrange them in a configuration that worked for her. Secondly, the water had shifted from being a threat to being life-giving. I spoke of the dual aspects of water—that it is a symbol both of life and of destruction, both womb and tomb, both to be revered and feared. It was my feeling that the water represented the deepest part of self—that place to which she could journey and find new life, if she would only choose to do so. Whether this interpretation was valid or not would surface in future sessions of image guidance and in the context of Elizabeth's own life.

When she came for her next session, Elizabeth brought an image with her. Rather hesitantly, she described the image of a hamster climbing frantically around a wheel within a ball; its movement set the ball rolling at a dizzying pace, but the hamster continued its endless climb, as though incapable of slowing down.

"I'm not sure if we can do anything with this image," she apologized. "I mean, it is a bit ridiculous."

"Don't worry," I responded, "I've had people dialogue with a whole range of images—witches, princesses, rats, knights, ghouls, blocks of granite—you name it."

"So you're going to have me talk to the hamster?"

"Yes," I said, amused by her obvious discomfort. I had come to realize that Elizabeth's tendency to intellectualize was a potential disadvantage; "suspending disbelief" did not come easily to her.

I dimmed the lights, led her through relaxation techniques and then asked her to focus on the image.

"I can't see the hamster—just the wheel turning, spinning fast, blurring. The hamster is inside—I know that—but I can't see into the ball."

"Elizabeth, imagine you are the hamster, spinning in the ball. What does it feel like?"

"I feel sick, confused—the motion is so swift."

Seeing that she was really into the image and that she

had identified strongly with the hamster's plight, I asked her if the hamster could be trying to escape something.

"It's trying to escape the wheel."

"Isn't there a way out?"

"No. Not unless the wheel stops spinning. At first the hamster made the wheel spin but now it's spinning on its own. It's stuck. It feels scared. It wants a way out."

"Can you see anything else?"

"Yes. There's a hand with a pencil—it stops the wheel by inserting the pencil point into a hole in the ball. The hamster is frazzled—it looks as though it's been through a hurricane. It's wet and dripping with sweat. It still feels dizzy."

"Is it relieved to have stopped the spinning?"

"It stares at me without moving."

"Ask the hamster what it's looking for."

"It says, 'You.' "

"Ask it to explain," I instructed, sensing that we were moving into significant territory.

"It won't talk to me. But there's a rat—an upright kind of rat who looks as though he might talk to me."

"O.K., I'll be the rat and you be the hamster. Perhaps the hamster will talk to the rat."

"This is absurd," said Elizabeth, "I'm glad nobody can overhear this conversation. They'd think we're crazy."

"Elizabeth, focus on the imagery again. Remember, I'm the rat and you're the hamster. Here goes. Hamster, as you spin in waking life, is it possible that you have lost touch with yourself?"

"Possibly."

"Are there deeper issues—things that you might be running from?"

"I don't think so, Rat. I can't see the rat anymore—it's gone."

"Let's talk to the hand, then," I suggested. "Hand, why did you stop the wheel?"

"So the hamster could get out."

"Hand, why is the hamster running?"

"I don't know. Liz, the hand is my hand—I recognize it."

Abandoning my role as rat, I asked Elizabeth why the hamster was running from her.

"It's looking for me and running from me at the same time."

"Tell the hamster that this answer isn't specific enough."

"The hamster disappears—I can't see it anymore."

"O.K. Perhaps we came on too strongly. Let's be gentler this time. Invite the hamster back."

"It's back—it looks friendlier this time."

"Ask it what it wants to find."

"It tells me, 'you,' meaning me; it wants to know who I am. Now it disappears again but the wheel remains spinning."

"Tell the wheel that you have no desire to get in it, that you are not going to get in it. Can you say these words out loud?"

"No. I don't feel comfortable doing so—I'll say the words to myself. I hold the wheel in both my hands and I tell it to stop. I feel frustrated—I feel like I'm holding a child I want to shake so it will do what I want it to do."

"Command the wheel to stop spinning."

"I grab the wheel by a spoke, but it continues to spin and pull."

"Hold the wheel tightly; know you are in control. Hold it in both hands—"

"I tossed it," said Elizabeth excitedly; "I tossed it over my shoulder. I feel free of the wheel—I feel I can move on."

"Does the wheel have anything to tell you, Elizabeth?"

"It says I can move from anger to detachment, from

detachment to liberation. It says that it [the wheel] was unimportant and that I didn't have to be anxious. It says that I am the one in control of my life and that I don't have to be in a frantic spin. It says I need to slow down and to stop running. I need to concentrate on how to get out of this frenetic state and to stop focusing on how discontent I am. I need to toss the negative out of my life, just as I tossed the wheel."

As we processed our session, several interesting insights surfaced. We both recognized what a struggle the session had been. The disappearing images and their reluctance to speak seemed to reflect Elizabeth's resistance to the process; though she had volunteered as subject and though she had an intellectual interest in image guidance, she was basically skeptical about its potential. In fact, she found the whole idea of dialoguing with images to be embarrassing. Faced with this resistance, I had become far more directive than I usually am as guide, forcing Elizabeth to confront the imagery in any way that seemed to have possibility. The breakthrough had happened just before we finished the session, when she had tossed the wheel without having received any directive to do so. Elizabeth experienced this moment as a transition from being stuck in the wheel to having the freedom to allow change to happen. She realized that a change in attitude can facilitate a change in external events; this, in turn, led her not only to try to change her negativity but also to bring about concrete adjustments in her lifestyle. She experienced the session as an invitation to stop her cycle of negativity and constant activity, so that she could begin the journey inward—that journey which had been symbolized by the water she had encountered in our first session together.

She began to take a serious look at her posture toward life, realizing that she was very much a spectator who judged those around her for their inadequacies while refusing to fully participate in life herself. Her habit of skipping classes and getting through by excelling in exams, her excessive frustration with the present moment while she looked forward to the future, and her very full schedule all indicated that she, like the hamster, was spinning at full speed. She needed to slow down and to look inward. In some ways, being confined to a wheelchair offered her the vantage point of detached critic of the outer world but also provided her with the excuse to avoid taking an inner inventory.

Our subsequent session plunged her deeply into her own spiritual journey. In the course of our conversations, I had noted a general softening in Elizabeth's attitude, a desire to change, an openness to inner reality, a modification of her cynicism. She had another dream which she related to me in detail. It began with the front view of her car. There was a light behind the car, shining with such intensity that the whole interior was illuminated. As the light grew more and more brilliant, the car disappeared. Then the light became fire; then the fire became a pool of water into which a single drop fell, causing ripples to cover the surface of the pool. In the next segment, Elizabeth was standing in an elevator that was shaking violently, as though it were going to crash. Three other figures crouched close to the floor, as if in fear. I used this dream sequence as our starting point.

"I can see inside the elevator—I'm standing on the side with the buttons to the right. Three people are crouching in scale formation—shortest to tallest—in front of me. They are clinging to themselves as though they are afraid."

"Can you see their faces?"

"No, they are hooded. Their eyes are covered but I can see their noses and mouths."

"Elizabeth, focus on the tallest person. Ask it to stand and look at you and then to reveal its name."

"This person has scraggly white hair under the hood. I ask it who it is and it says—"

At this point, she began to laugh, as though barely able to believe what she was hearing.

"It says it's God," she spluttered.

"God," I repeated, taken by surprise.

"Ask God why God is afraid."

"Fears the world," said Elizabeth. Fully absorbed by what she was saying, I felt myself shiver.

"Why?"

"Because the world fears God."

"What does God mean by that?" I asked.

"No answer. God has kneeled down again and the other two also remain kneeling, but one of them seems taller than it did."

"Ask this second figure who it is."

"Friend." Again, I felt the electricity of her response; intuitively, I knew that this would be an encounter with a Christ-figure.

"Ask Friend why he has come to you," I instructed. There was a look of intense concentration on Elizabeth's face.

"I just get, 'am a part—a part of the whole.' "

"Ask Friend to explain what this means."

"I don't know if this is valid, Liz, but the words keep coming, 'I am the way, the truth and the life. . . .' They keep popping into my head and I wonder if I'm doing this. We were talking about religion before—"

"Do these words feel valid?"

"Yes, on a feeling level they feel real, but intellectually I don't know if I buy this. Now Friend reaches out his hand and I take it in mine—there's no hesitation. I simply take it, unable to resist. He is wearing monk's garb and all I can see is the hand and his forearm. I feel calm and surprised. Again, it all feels very real; in the dream, the elevator was shaking but everything is peaceful now."

"Elizabeth, call on the third person and ask that person to reveal who it is to you." As I gave her these instructions, I fully expected an encounter with the Holy Spirit would follow.

"As I let go of Friend's hand, I see the smallest person's face. The person is ugly and distorted. I'm not afraid of it but it is sort of frightening. It is more unpleasant than the other characters."

"Ask the person who it is," I said, abandoning my expectation of a Trinitarian encounter.

Elizabeth was convulsed with laughter. "It says it's me. It points at me with sarcasm, scoffing at me."

"Ask the ugly person why she is so ugly."

"She just keeps pointing at me, staring and ugly. She just keeps staring at me and pointing. She's got dark eyes. I think she's an image of my negativity."

"Ask—"

"Liz, I just kicked her. I kicked her because she was making me mad. She's stubborn so I kicked her. She became like a gnome so I bowled her over. (Laughter) Now she lies on the ground—now she's disappeared. The other two people are left, but she's disappeared."

"Ask Friend what you need to do," I said. By this time, I was feeling profoundly moved; the room was charged with the presence of otherness, and keeping the process going had become radically difficult.

"Friend seems to need help. He says—'Follow me, I need help. . . .' "

"Ask Friend what he needs help for."

"I keep thinking in universal terms, Liz. The words I hear are 'The world' and 'Tell them.' "

"Tell them what?"

"It won't tell me."

"Ask God what you're meant to do."

"God turned his back on me but he said—this sounds like a Nike commercial—'JUST DO IT.' I've become a black spot on the floor."

"Ask the black spot what you're meant to say," I instructed. By this point, I wanted the full revelation—all of it. It was as though I were a religious devotee, listening to a sacred oracle. I was not yet ready to bring the session to a close.

"The black circle has become a giant human eye. Light comes from the eye—a misty light. Beams of light strike the ground and this causes the misty effect. The light says, 'Tell them who you are.' "

"What do you understand by that, Elizabeth?"

"I'm not getting anything—the images have left."

"O.K. Let's forget the images. What do you, Elizabeth, understand by these words?"

"I don't know—I'll have to think about it. I keep getting the idea that I'm shouting back at them, saying, 'I'm just me!' and they say, 'No, but you're more.' "

"What is it they mean?"

"That's all—there's nothing more."

We sat in silence, awed by the images and by the words they had spoken. When I asked Elizabeth if she were confused, she said she was filled with wonder. She remembered how easy it had been to have a relationship with God when she was a child—blind faith was so simple. Now, as an adult, she couldn't claim to have a relationship of any sort with God. And yet, in spite of this, she had been completely ready to follow Friend; her heart drew her toward him; her head told her to proceed with caution. She was intrigued by her treatment of the gnome. Spontaneously, she had kicked it, just as she had tossed the frenetic wheel. Her instincts, then, were to move toward life and away from negativity. As to responding to the "Call" she had received from Friend, she needed time to process this on her own. For both of us, the session had provided more than we had bargained for.

It was almost two months later before we rescheduled. The Christmas season, an attack of flu and a snowstorm all played their part in delaying the next meeting. When we did finally get together, I was aware that there was something profoundly different about Elizabeth. The rough edges were gone; I no longer detected the cynicism that had been so apparent before. There had also been a softening of Elizabeth's expression; her face seemed fuller, more alive. As we prepared for our image work, I questioned her about these changes. With some embarrassment, she explained that she no longer felt the need to criticize people and that she therefore felt better inside. She attributed this shift to our previous image guidance session which had left her feeling very peaceful. I shared with her the powerful impact the session had on me and suggested that since she had not brought in any specific images, we could re-enter the last image experience.

As usual, I darkened the room and invited her to relax. When she seemed to be completely still, I asked her to see again the figures in the elevator.

"I can just see Friend," she said, "only now he is wearing a monk's white garb. I can't see his face—it's black in the center—but for some reason, I think he's smiling. He looks at his fingers as though he's thinking about something, but it's nothing too heavy."

"Does he greet you?"

"Not exactly—but he smiles and this makes me smile," said Elizabeth, her face breaking into a smile.

"How are you feeling?" I asked.

"Good," responded Elizabeth in a tone which suggested that I had asked the obvious.

"Is there anything you want to ask him—perhaps why he's smiling?"

"O.K. He says he's proud of me."

"Does he say why?"

"I'm getting something like I'm doing what he intends—I'm becoming what he intended."

"What do you understand by that?"

"I'm trying to ask him," said Elizabeth, a little impatiently. Her forehead creased over and she was silent for a few minutes. "I'm getting the word 'instrument.' "

Again, there was a period of silence; the look of intense concentration returned.

"He's turned around now—"

"Did you ask about 'instrument?' "

"I'm afraid—"

"Why don't you ask?" I persisted. "You can always say no to him."

"I have to get his attention again—I'll invite him back. Now he's holding out his hand."

"That's the only response?"

"Yes."

"Are there any questions you want to ask him?"

"I feel like I shouldn't ask right now—it's the kind of feeling you can get when you're talking to a close friend and there are some things you don't ask because you know the answers."

"What does it feel like to hold his hand?"

"I can't describe it—but did you ever hear of the highest state of consciousness for Hindus where there's just nothing? It's a good feeling. . . ."

"Elizabeth, stay with the feeling. Concentrate on being with Friend. Don't feel that you have to repeat back anything. Focus on the feeling."

"We've just gone from holding hands to walking—I can

only see—I feel it's me, that he's behind me. You know how someone stands behind you and puts his arms around you? It's like that. There's just light. . . . I know this sounds weird . . . when I went to Boston, I was standing on a cliff, looking at the ocean at sunset . . . it's where I am just now. It's good to be here . . . he's still holding me. . . ."

"Is there anything you want to say to him?" I asked.

"No—it would ruin everything. Now we're at the edge of the cliff. We're separate. I'm swinging my legs back and forth over the edge. . . . I'm not afraid to fall off, but he wants me to jump over."

At that, she frowned; I remembered her fear of water and wondered how this would affect her decision.

"We've jumped. We're holding hands as we go down. We've landed in the water—the same water as the water in that first dream—it's so dark. . . ."

"Are you afraid?"

"No—apprehensive would be a better word. Now he's gone. I've come up to the top, gasping for air. The sun is still setting. I want to get out of the water. . . ."

"Can you?"

"No—the cliff is so straight-edged that there's no way out. . . ."

"So what do you do?"

"Well, I'm just sitting there in the water—I can't remember the name of it—oh yes, treading water, but I don't feel tired. I feel I can do it forever. . . . Now I see him again. There's a beach and I'm swimming toward it, but it keeps fading away. Friend is there—he reaches out for me—he's on land and I'm still in the water. Now I've gotten to him and he's pulling me out of the water. He gives me a hug but I can't see anything more—he's gone. . . ."

"How are you feeling?"

"I feel I've gone from one extreme to another. First I

felt peaceful, then anxious and apprehensive in the water, and now I'm content and peaceful again."

"Stay in this consciousness for as long as you want, Elizabeth," I instructed. "Thank Friend for being with you. Tell Friend anything you may want to say to him. Then when you are ready, open your eyes slowly and we will talk about what has happened."

When we processed the session, Elizabeth described how afraid she had been in the water and the feeling she had that she was going to drown. "As I trod water, I became more at ease," she explained. "When I first hit the water, I was terrified, but I knew what I had to do." What had impressed her even more than this, however, was the experience of Friend coming up behind her and hugging her. "I literally felt him behind me—it was so real it was creepy. It was also funny how he kept on making me smile—every time I saw his smile I was ready to start giggling. I couldn't restrain the smile—I just had to grin. It was a killer smile—the kind you have to smile back to. There were no eyes or ears—it was too dark under the cowl—only the smile."

One of my observations was that Elizabeth no longer offered critical commentary during the process. "At times I wondered if I should really say what I was seeing and whether it would sound stupid, but somehow I was able to go along with the process. My friends would just be amazed—I used to be so cynical. . . ."

"And where does all this leave you?" I asked.

"I don't know—"

"That's not an acceptable response after a powerful session," I retorted.

"Well, something's bothering me . . . there's a missing piece that I don't quite get. . . ."

"Elizabeth, I believe it has something to do with your response, with your relationship to Friend; I think it has something to do with commitment, but that is for you to explore. He will always reach out to you, but you need to do the swimming toward the beach or you will stay stuck, treading water. . . ."

The next time we met, Elizabeth brought in a dream that had disturbed her and asked if we could process it. She had dreamed she had gone fishing with her sister, Maureen, but whereas she enjoyed fishing in waking life, Elizabeth found herself repulsed by her dream experience. As usual, she did the fishing while Maureen removed the fish from the hook. But while in waking life Maureen would toss the fish back into the water, in the dream she scraped out their eyes before doing so. The fish didn't bleed as a result of this treatment, but they did seem to swim rather aimlessly, once they were back in the water. Elizabeth noticed that the dream ego (that is, the figure she recognized to be herself in the dream) was upset at her sister's actions, but, nevertheless, she continued to fish and did not intervene on their behalf.

Before moving into image guidance, I asked Elizabeth to draw a picture of the most dominant symbol; this she identified to be the fish. I handed her crayons and watched as she colored in the crude form of a silver fish. Then I asked her to dialogue with the fish. I suggested several questions she could ask and instructed her to write down whatever responses came to her, without censoring them for content or grammar. Through this exercise, she learned that she was angry with Maureen for being so cruel, and that she was also angry with herself for not being able to help the fish. It seemed that the dream images were inviting her to let go of behavior that was in some way irresponsible and hurtful to others. We talked about her tendency in waking life to be critical of others. Elizabeth felt that she had dealt with this trait effectively and was surprised that it should reappear in her dreams. We decided to test dream meaning through image guidance.

I led Elizabeth through relaxation exercises and then asked her to focus on the image of a fish, swimming close to the shore. Like the fish in her dream, it was silver and eyeless. "Ask the fish, 'What have you come to tell me?' " I said. "Then listen to its response."

"The fish says it's bringing a warning."

"What kind of warning?"

"Of things to come."

"What does it mean by that?"

"It says, 'If you catch us (meaning the fish) you can't send us away mindlessly and blind.' "

"Why not?"

"Because soon they'll all be blind if I continue my fishing, and they'll be as blind as the world."

"What does that mean to you?"

"That when I catch a fish I need to teach it so that it can avoid Maureen—so it can avoid being injured."

"Is that it?" I asked, surprised at the terseness of the message. My question was greeted by silence, so I invited Elizabeth to ask the fish what it represented.

"Future minds," she said. "And it says to understand the fish, if you can let it go. . . ."

"How do you interpret that?" I was beginning to feel frustrated with the fish's obscurity.

"Well, I could apply it to my disability in that if someone can understand me, then they can look at other disabled people in another light."

"What kind of light?"

"Just in the sense of empathy instead of pity. With a different kind of understanding. . . ."

"Ask the fish if there's anything you're doing now that is harmful, if there's anything you need to change."

"Just that I'm sending the fish away blind," said Elizabeth. "I assume it means that I'm not teaching them."

"Ask what you should be teaching them."

"I don't know."

"Do you remember the image of Friend?"

"Yes. Of course."

"Remember Friend the way you last saw him. Ask Friend what it is you are meant to be teaching."

"Teaching about Friend, teaching about myself. . . ."

"Ask what is stopping you from doing that."

"I think that if I don't take the fish off the hook, then Maureen will get to them first and make them blind. But I hate touching fish—I would much rather have Maureen touch them. But in order to intervene, I would have to take them off the hook."

"And then you would teach them?"

"Yes."

"Is there anything else you need to ask Friend?"

"Just maybe to help me know how to take the fish off the hook. Maybe to give me the courage to do it. . . ."

"Can you ask him to help you?"

"He says I have the answers within myself."

"Elizabeth, you do have the answers within yourself," I said. "Spend some time thinking about what that means and then we'll talk about what you have learned."

After a period of silence, Elizabeth opened her eyes. She again mentioned her cynical mask and realized that some of it still lingered. "But there's a good side to it," she insisted. "I can make people laugh. Being sarcastic is part of my personality—I actually enjoy it."

"Being sarcastic for fun is one thing," I countered, "but when it becomes a mask to hide the real self from those we deal with, then there's a problem. You have to decide when the sarcasm is a mask or when it's not."

"Well, it is useful at times," Elizabeth insisted. "I don't always want to face my issues. At times I would rather put on a head set or watch TV. Wearing a mask allows me to escape my problems some of the time. Usually, I am able to go back to my issues, when I want to. Though it's true that I sometimes forget to do this. . . ."

I suggested that Elizabeth should pay more attention to her cynical mask and that she should notice the ways in which she used it; only then would she know if her words or actions were having a harmful effect on others.

It was several months before I saw Elizabeth again. During that time, I had gone to Europe and back, and she had had major surgery to correct her posture. It had been a long, painful summer for her, but she had begun to feel the benefits of the surgery and was glad to be back on campus once more. The whole experience of the surgery had made her feel somewhat separated from her old images. She had resumed a busy schedule but noted that she had not fallen into the old, frenetic patterns. Cynicism remained distant and, instead, she found herself looking forward to graduate school. In contrast to previous terms, she was now attending class regularly and was keeping up with assignments. She realized that she was at a new level of acceptance in terms of being confined to a wheelchair: "At first, it used to be a question of looking at what I could no longer do and what I had to do; now I have a new level of confidence and hopefulness. If people try to avoid my disability, I tend to force them to notice it, so that I can get all the assistance I sometimes need—access to a building, for example, or a guaranteed parking space."

The image we worked with was an image of the sun, suspended in darkness, radiating great light all around it. As she moved more deeply into her image, I asked Elizabeth where she saw herself in relation to the sun.

"In its intensity, brightness and power, I see it as an image of myself—of my soul, if you will."

"Ask the sun why it shines so brightly in the darkness," I instructed. Elizabeth frowned in concentration. "Because of the power within which allows it to overcome the darkness," was her response.

"Ask the sun where the power comes from," I said, feeling that we had come to a significant moment in our process.

"When you said that, I knew it comes from my heart," she said, gesturing toward her chest. "It's a feeling of being uplifted, of real excitement about something—everything seems new."

"Where does the heart's power come from?"

"I don't know. I just know it's there. I have a deep feeling of well-being, perhaps because the physical and spiritual are so intertwined."

"Ask the sun/soul where the power comes from," I said.

"I'm just getting, 'it is.' It's simply there."

"Ask the sun/soul what you need to do to make this power grow."

"It's growing as you speak—almost as if it has no bounds because there are so many directions in which it can grow. It has no limits. It's been in hibernation for a very long time. The image reminds me of a children's book: the sun went away into its house; all the animals need the sun to come out, and, after a very long time, it does come out and there is great rejoicing. Slowly, the sun comes out of the doors and the light is almost indescribable."

"So the light has come because you need it and others need it?" I observed.

"I'm content for a change. I feel more substantial, better about myself because others need me. I don't feel as though I need people as much as they seem to need me. I sense that I now have a function, a purpose for others. I need to see myself mirrored in their eyes before I can have feelings of self-acceptance."

"Ask the sun/soul why it has taken so long to come out."

"It's almost as if I had to rediscover it," said Elizabeth, "because I'd forgotten about it. I don't know why it disappeared in the first place."

"Why don't you ask it?"

"It seems that other things tended to have more importance, and other things overshadowed the sun and soon it was so overshadowed that it was forgotten altogether."

"Ask the sun why it came back."

"Because I allowed it to come back," said Elizabeth.

"You wanted it to come back?"

"Right. I needed it to come back. All the things that blocked it out in the first place were negative things that were eating away at me, but I didn't need these things. They were unnecessary."

"I know that you feel distant from the old images, but see if Friend comes back to you. What does he think about all this?"

"I see his arms. The sun is in his hands."

"What does this mean?"

"I don't know. I just know it's there. Now he reaches out and gives me the sun."

"Ask Friend what he wants of you."

"He needs me to take care of the sun and to polish it up once in a while so that it keeps its glow. I guess you could say my soul needs constant maintenance."

"How can you take care of your soul?"

"By doing the right thing when I know it's the right thing. I guess just by knowing it's there to maintain and that I have to do it. He's giving it to me again—"

"What do you see?"

"He handed it to me and I took it from him. Sort of like he's establishing that it's mine to take care of, even though there are times when he holds it for me. All of a sudden, I feel as though he has placed this big responsibility on me. I feel burdened. The first thing that comes to mind is that I have all these things to do—but I have to set priorities. It was because I failed to do this that I lost the sun in the first place. I wasn't aware of the sun/soul. I wasn't mature enough, so it went away."

"Ask Friend if he can help you carry the burden of your soul/sun."

"He says that whenever I feel overwhelmed, I can give it back to him for a while, instead of putting it away. Someone must be responsible for it at all times—if it is not me, it had better be Friend."

Elizabeth shivered slightly. "See. I'm covered in goosebumps. What do you think caused this?"

"Perhaps it's the intensity of the experience," I suggested. "The imagery has been very powerful, and there's much for you to process. Why don't you spend a few minutes gazing at the shining soul/sun, and then, when you're ready, we can talk about the experience."

When Elizabeth had returned to waking consciousness, we were both aware of how easily she had moved into her sun image, even though we hadn't worked together in several months. Though she was not conscious of having paid much attention to her inner life during the weeks in the hospital, it was evident that "movement" had been happening beneath the surface. She was centered, joyful and optimistic; she felt better about herself and was making decisions about the future. The sun image reflected all of this. She had found inner peace and that had made all the difference—for herself, for those around her and for those she would work with in the future. . . .

As we continued to work together, it became increasingly apparent to me that God was calling her to greater intimacy and to a healthier lifestyle. I sensed resistance on Elizabeth's part—disbelief that God could want anything of her or that she would have anything to give, perhaps. Over and over again, the images called her to examine her own life of faith; and, consistently, Elizabeth seemed torn between wanting to respond and wanting to continue on with the old patterns of doing things—patterns of partying and speeding, of not taking care of her physical needs, of being almost indifferent to her safety.

She came in to see me one afternoon with the news that she might be facing more major surgery—this time to correct a loop of scar tissue, left from three previous surgeries, which was causing digestive problems. Intuitively, I felt that the surgery could be avoided and decided to test this during our time together.

"Focus on the scar tissue," I said. "It needs a name. Perhaps you can name it for me."

At first, Elizabeth frowned, finding it difficult to concentrate on something as unappealing as scar tissue. "We'll call it ST," she said. "It's gross looking—I'm trying to think of a way to describe it. It's not exactly bubbly or oozy, but it reminds me a little of what the brain looks like."

"What's it doing?"

"It's just strangling my insides—now it's grown over all of my stomach and it's growing all over the rest of my body, too."

"What else is happening?"

"It's wrapped itself around my wrists" (Elizabeth squeezed her hands together in discomfort). "I pull at it but it won't break."

"So it's tying all of you up?"

"Yes. I feel like I want to struggle with it, but at the same time, I don't care."

"Why is that?" I asked, feeling my intuitive hunch grow stronger.

"I don't know. Struggling with it would be exhausting at this point. It would be futile because it's engulfed me. It's covered me from head to toe—I'm cocooned in it, almost."

"How do you feel?"

"Uh, it's not a good feeling. I don't feel very safe but I sense that there will be some metamorphosis—but it will take outside intervention."

"How will this metamorphosis happen?"

"Something will have to make a cut from the outside."

"Like a doctor?"

"No. I guess I would need something worthwhile to make me want to come out of the cocoon. The scarring seems to represent more than a physical state, after all. There is all the emotional scarring that has been going on for such a long time. Does this make sense?"

"Yes," I said, feeling even more strongly that surgery was not the answer to Elizabeth's digestive problems. "Can you say any more about this?"

"Well, there's everything that's happened over the last four years—a sense of loss, having to cope with a new situation. I'm left feeling scared, but it's not a hopeless situation."

"So the question is, what is the new life that's waiting for you? O.K. Imagine yourself breaking out of the cocoon—"

"I told you, I can't do this unless there's an initial cut from the outside."

"Ask the cocoon how this can happen," I instructed.

"Liz, hands have just opened up the cocoon. . . ."

"Whose?"

"I don't know—the cocoon is open and I'm looking out of a large hole. . . ."

"What do you see?"

"A figure standing there. . . ."

"Can you describe the figure?"

"Well, I recognize the hands—they're the same hands I've seen in every one of our sessions together."

"Friend's?" I asked, knowing full well what the response would be.

"Yes," said Elizabeth, laughing with embarrassment.

"Do you see Friend?"

"Yes—well, not really, because I don't see his face. I haven't come out yet."

"What are you waiting for?"

"I don't know . . . nothing special . . . now I'm not waiting for anything at all. . . ."

"Ask Friend why he wants you to come out."

"I don't know so much that he wants me to come out as he wants me to make a choice."

"About what?"

"Well, to put it simply, he either wants me to come out or to stay in."

"Does he speak to you?"

"No, he never speaks to me, but I just know what he wants me to hear."

"What is there to be gained by staying in the cocoon?"

"Nothing I can see—but I guess it wouldn't take any effort to stay put."

"What is to be gained by leaving?"

"I—oh, he's just said something to me—I don't know where this came from—something like I should be ashamed to die before I have done my part."

"Does that surprise you?"

"No."

"What does it mean to you?"

"I don't know," said Elizabeth, looking flustered.

"It sounds as though you have some task to do. Does that excite you at all?"

"No it doesn't," she said emphatically.

"What would you like to do?"

"Nothing. I'm just so tired. I would like to stay in the cocoon—isn't that terrible? But if I stay in the cocoon, I will be ashamed."

"Being ill gives you the opportunity to stay in the cocoon, doesn't it?"

"Yes, it gives me a convenient excuse."

"Ask Friend how you can find healing for your stomach."

"He says I know what I need to do, and he's right."

"What is that?"

"I just need to take care of myself."

"How?"

"I don't know how and that's the problem. I feel I'm going in circles. . . ."

"Ask Friend how to go about doing it."

"He won't tell me because I know the answer already."

"Elizabeth, tell me what you need to do."

"I need to be eating properly and sleeping more. I should stop living on alcohol and pop. But I hate constraints on my behavior. . . ."

"So the surgery would allow you to carry on with your present lifestyle?"

"Yes."

"Ask Friend what his response is to all this."

"Disappointment."

"With?"

"Me. I don't think he sees any worth in what I've done."

"Do you see any worth?"

"Sometimes. I think Friend thinks there's some worth in what I've done but that there's much more that needs doing. . . . I'm not hearing anything else."

"What's your response to this?"

"I just don't believe him."

"Can you see his hands still?"

"Yes."

"What do they look like?"

"They're different every time. They're rough and calloused this time. Tired, but not ugly."

"Do you think that perhaps they need your help?"

"Like soaking them in Palmolive?"

"No," I said. "Like sharing in the work."

"Perhaps."

"You sound non-committal."

"I'm always non-committal."

"Why?"

"I just am. I guess it's a character flaw."

"So it's not something you're proud of?"

"No."

"Has anything else happened?"

"There's been no resolution, but at the same time, there's an understanding, a give and take kind of thing."

"And what is the understanding?"

"That if he doesn't push me, I might do something for him."

"How does that leave you feeling?"

"I feel I'm back at square #1."

"With ST throttling your stomach?"

Elizabeth laughed. "No. I feel his disappointment."

"What are you going to do about it?"

"Did I ever tell you that I came out of the cocoon?"

"No, you didn't. So this whole argument with Friend took place on the outside?"

"Yes."

"Are you going back in?"

"No. You should see it. It's really grotesque—like something out of a really bad horror movie."

"So you just wanted to face him and that was enough to get you out?"

"Yes."

"Now what?"

"I took his hand a while back and I could feel how rough it was. But mine are just as rough as his."

"Is your hand still in his?"

"Yes."

"And you still feel his disappointment?"

"Yes—this hurts me more than being angry with him."

"Why are you angry with him?"

"It's a defense. I'm angry at his audacity."

"Does he understand?"

"I don't think he cares—not about me, I mean, but the way that I feel."

"What does he care about?"

"I just feel it would make him completely happy if I didn't question at all and just did what he wanted."

"Which is?"

"I don't know."

"You *really* don't know?"

"I guess it would be to live his way in general."

"And what would that mean?"

"Well, I feel he's telling me I'm not a good person—" Suddenly, she burst out laughing, realizing that she had put her hands on her hips in a confrontational stance.

"I see you're indignant."

"Yes," she spluttered. "I want to have the final word. . . ."

"Elizabeth, look at Friend. See him standing before

you, waiting for you, wanting your friendship. Listen to what he has to say to you. Respond, if you wish, and then, when you are ready, open your eyes."

The words Elizabeth heard were, "It will all come to a good end." What she understood by this was that when she would eventually look back on her life, she would see that everything she had gone through was somehow necessary. Friend would be patient with her, but there were conscious choices which she needed to make when she was ready.

Elizabeth's Response to Image Guidance

I was enveloped in an endless pattern of empty days and nights, concentrating more on what my life lacked than the promise it held. Physically, I was slowly deteriorating. Bouts of nausea accompanied by vomiting developed into a possible peptic ulcer. I was tired and it seemed as though I just could not get enough sleep. My days were primarily spent in bed; as a result, skipping classes became a norm. I blamed the missed classes on my physical state, while ignoring the fact that my attitude had been the problem all the while.

My mental state had gone from bad to worse. I was in a hurry to finish my undergraduate studies and move on. I did not want any part of the situation in which I had found myself, nor any part of the people who were around me. The interpersonal relationships that already existed in my life were suffering. My bad attitude warranted constant complaints from those who were closest to me. This, coupled with the unrelenting illness, finally woke me up to how serious the situation had become.

The negativity I was experiencing was born from frustration—frustration with the stagnant situation I had found myself in. I was desperate to find an escape and, as a result, I threw myself into a frenzy of activity. I was essentially grasping at straws, looking for an alternative. It was about this time that I received Liz's request for volunteers.

My initial reaction to the process of image guidance was one of apprehension. I was wary of the process itself, but even more so of the truths it would uncover. Nevertheless, the process seemed to be the best candidate to replace the confusing array of activities I had undertaken. I had difficulty at first, due mostly to my general skepticism and denial of everything affirmed or suggested by others. Yet, as the sessions progressed, I found myself to be more at ease with the process and more understanding about the way in which it worked. With Liz's guidance accented by my over-active imagination, I was soon able to plunge into my inner self.

A daydreamer by trade, I was not surprised by how accessible the unconscious mind is, nor by the very natural way in which I was received in the world of images, throughout my journeying. Yet, to my surprise and delight came the realization that the messages of the unconscious are somewhat prophetic in nature and are worthy of consideration in regard to one's life experiences.

The images I dialogued with were representatives of the negative aspects of my life—aspects I felt were uncontrollable. I soon discovered that these negative images existed because I had allowed them to exist. For a long time, I had blamed my miserable state on external causes, forgetting that one is essentially ruled by one's own heart and mind. I came to understand that people and things are more inclined to react to you than act upon you. This change of heart I was experiencing came easily through the image process as I was able to place concepts like frustration and confusion into a physical form.

Being able to view the concepts of negativity in concrete form (e.g. a spinning wheel) enabled me to deal with issues more effectively. By examining the concepts as something tangible, I was able to get a physical grasp on the situation and to create change in my mind. In turn, the process was empowering as this change flowed over into my life. My part, as I saw it, was to become an actor in my own life—a promoter of the positive instead of a catalyst for the seemingly infectious negativity that plagued me.

The act of discovery is part of what image work is about. I discovered it was I who made the list on which my inner self was least important. I realized the power of change came from within. For example, one may be physically static within one's station in life, but one does not need to remain in that state mentally or spiritually. As obvious as this revelation may seem to most, it came to me as a surprise in the midst of my hopelessness.

The images armed me with the knowledge that I was in control and that I was the keeper of my own soul. It was then that I began to weed out all that was negative in me and in my life. The process did not occur overnight; in fact, I suspect it will continue for some time. Still, as slowly as the negativity crept into my life, it began to retreat. Not only did my mental state begin to improve, but my physical health did as well. Most importantly, I have accepted the responsibility for the events in my life and feel that I have some control over them.

Image guidance has also helped me to understand my present self and to see how what I have become has its roots in the past. In one session, I pictured three icebergs in order from largest to smallest. The larger two had large roots which plunged deep into the sea. The roots reminded me of dragnets picking up the waste from the ocean floor. These icebergs moved along at the same pace and along the same conventional path—slicing through the icy water with the consistency of time itself. The smallest iceberg, while equivalent to the others in mass, was lacking both height and depth. This iceberg, which I came to identify as a representation of myself, had no root. It had only a simple base about a foot thick. Being rootless, the little one was able to move much faster than the other two cumbersome icebergs. Basically, it had no "baggage" (no dragnet full of debris) to lug around, so it was not burdened by the roots that throttled the others. And although the little one traveled in the same general direction as the others, it seemed to take small detours, following closely for a while and then jetting out in another direction, only to return to the safety of the procession. It was because this little iceberg traveled without precision that it needed to keep up its faster rate. I suspected its need to escape the mundane, as it deviated from the others, was a matter of experience. Bravely breaking away to gain new forms of knowledge but forming no attachment to any of the various outlets, it returned to the ceremonial parade. It seemed to have an insatiable appetite for the extraordinary, but still looked to the others for direction.

Liz commented that the way in which the iceberg traveled was perhaps a metaphor for the way in which I traveled through life—following those that are oppressed by their dragnets (their roots) and refusing to commit myself to any form of leadership role. In this context, the image seemed to be a re-emergence of an earlier image—one that challenged me to take a position as a guide in life instead of as an observer. If this conjecture is valid, then the message seems to be another challenge. Instead of hurrying frantically to keep up with the others, I need to set the pace and risk leaving the cumbersome others behind (they may be unable to follow because they cannot let go of their restricting roots that are firmly fixed to the "straight and narrow" path).

The discussion of the bottomless iceberg prompted the same question from Liz that I had experienced from family, friends and psychologists over the last four years. However, in this context, the question related to the root of my iceberg. Why had I not placed all of the "baggage" that I had accumulated as a result of my accident at the base of my iceberg? Instead of a generic "I don't know"—used in an effort to conceal the deeper part of myself—I took a risk and answered. The answer I gave—an answer I had never shared before—is as confusing to me as it is embarrassing to narrate now.

Years previous to my injury, as I lay in bed at night—sleepless—I would occasionally imagine that a tragedy of some kind had occurred and, as a result, I was left paralyzed. Sometimes, I would carry out my "play" to the point of actually dragging my upper body along the bed, with my pseudo-immobile legs in tow, all the time suffering to the point of weeping. Not being a dramatic child but very much a realist, I wrote off these episodes as pure fantasy. I did not realize at the age of thirteen that I was obviating some of the future pain I was to experience five years later.

As I look back, I recognize that the feeling of "loss" was the only real thing about my experience. I know that my childhood imaginings cannot compare with the "nothingness" that presently generates from my lower body. And it cannot compare with the pure shock an eighteen year old experiences when faced with the knowledge that life will cease to exist as he or she knows it. Still, while the experience could not imitate or fully equate with life immediately following my injury or with life as I know it now, it did have an after-effect: it mirrored the "distress" that was yet to come. So when the time came and the immediate shock had lifted, all that was left seemed somewhat familiar to me and soon it became all that I knew. Having suffered through the loss of my legs before it became a reality, I was able to move quickly from a period of suffering into a time of learning—learning not only about my new physique, but also about my new world view.

I had moved into the stage of learning quickly enough not to have collected and stored all the anger and resentment one might find at the root of their iceberg. The "baggage"—the root of the iceberg—had been dealt with through play and premonition, and had broken away in my mind long before it had even existed in my life. This saved me from the time most people spend filling their dragnets, allowing me to be free enough to explore the unchartered waters of my life.

Left alone in the world of images, I may have wandered recklessly. It was nice to have someone who could add comfort to the journey and objectivity to the interpretation process. Liz was able to guide me into what I could only describe as the depths of my soul—going beyond the dust that had lingered there so long and drawing into the light all the beauty, courage and love that had always been there and which I sorely missed. Through the process, I not only learned to trust in myself again, but I learned to trust in another.

Image Guidance and Stress-Related Illnesses

These days, it is widely accepted that there are links between the way we feel about ourselves and our state of health, between our life experiences and our life expectancy. Often, the onset of serious illness corresponds to a period of great stress in a person's life. This is not to say that all chronically ill people have brought on their own conditions, but, in many cases, our illnesses do arise out of the major traumas we experience. I recently clipped a tragic entry from the *Chicago Tribune.* It referred to a child who, at six weeks, was severely beaten by his father and was left with 26 rib fractures, 8 leg fractures, a fractured right foot and a one inch tear in his ear; now, a year later, the child has what the newspaper described as "unrelated terminal liver cancer." Upon reading this, I found myself angrily saying, "Of course it's related—anyone can see that!" My immediate response was conditioned by a lifetime of knowing people who have suffered from stress-related illnesses. I remembered a high school friend whose menstrual period had stopped for more than a year after her boyfriend had broken up with her. I thought of another friend's newborn baby who ended up being hospitalized for failure to thrive symptoms which an astute doctor attributed to a "nervous environment" created by the child's well-meaning but interfering grandmother. I thought, too, of a close friend, devastated by lupus, whose intense rage had seemingly taken on a life of its own and was succeeding in destroying her. And I remembered a neighbor who more or less willed herself to die after the death of her husband, as well as my own children's pattern of "getting sick" when school became intolerable to them. Within my own limited experience, then, I have been connected to people whose bodies have responded to stress by getting ill. In looking back on my own life, I also have to admit that I can see distinct patterns where anything from headaches to gynecological disorders (some involving major surgery) had precipitating causes in my emotional life.

Though I cannot scientifically prove the relationship between illness and stress, I know that our life scripts and the images we carry within ourselves can work for our benefit or for our destruction. It is no coincidence that at those times when we are most over-extended we come down with colds and other minor ailments. It is no coincidence that people suffering from major loss (the loss of a spouse, for example, or the loss of a job) often develop serious medical conditions. It is a wise medical doctor who looks for underlying causes before treating the outer symptoms. It is a wise spiritual guide who sees body-mind-spirit connections and is able to work for the healing of the whole person.

It was in the middle of a spiritual direction session that I decided image guidance might be of use to Dan. I had been seeing Dan, a Catholic seminarian, for about six months; during that time, he had developed a mysterious ailment which afflicted his right arm. He was often in acute pain and was unable to use it for the ordinary activities of writing, playing the piano and driving. Limited in what he could do, he felt frustrated and out of control. I was aware that the mystery ailment loomed larger in his consciousness than any-thing else—even ordination. He was frightened of the life-long implications of his condition, particularly as the medical establishment had been unable to help him. After hand X-rays, bone scans, blood tests, C-T scans, an EMG and an MRI, neither he nor his doctors were any the wiser as to what was going on. I sensed that it was pointless trying to deal with spiritual issues when his mind was firmly centered on his disability.

I asked him if he could identify any images which would help me understand how he felt about his condition.

"Well, I feel as thought I have been zapped by a light-ning bolt—I can't see my hand—it has vanished from the elbow down, which was where the lightning bolt struck. It also feels as though a giant paper clasp has gripped my arm, but again, I can't see the arm itself. Or it feels as though a huge jaw has chomped down on my wrist—like in 'Jaws,' the movie."

"You are describing externalized pain. Is there any image which will let me understand how you feel on the inside?"

"Yes. I feel boxed in. Helpless. Squashed in. The lid is heavy and there's no way of raising it."

"Let's start with the image of you in the box. I'm going to lead you through some relaxation exercises, and then I will ask you to focus on the image. As I ask you questions, try to answer them without opening your eyes. If, for some reason, the going gets rough, then let me know and we can stop the process. . . ."

When Dan seemed thoroughly relaxed, I asked him to describe what he could see.

"A skeleton in a womb. Anguished. All is black. My knees are crunched, my back is bent. I'm tense, insecure, breathing fast, panting. . . ."

"How do you feel on the inside?"

"I'm in panic. I feel helpless. I'm rocking and whimpering. I've a feeling of unending desperation. . . ."

"It doesn't sound as though you are very happy. . . . Ask the box how you got inside."

"Box, how did I get inside you? It says, 'You walked in. You volunteered. You let yourself be hurt. Your fear is what keeps you from having enough power to lift the lid. I'm going to feed on your fears and powerlessness as long as you want me to. I am evil and want to hold you in here. A long time ago, you thought you could get out, but you gave up too soon. You were closer then than you have been at any other point.' "

As he spoke, Dan seemed immersed in pain. I could tell that he was having difficulty facing this inner voice, but I felt he would benefit from staying with the pain.

"Ask the box how you can escape," I instructed.

"Box, how can I escape? It says, 'You can dissolve my walls but I won't tell you how. You can unlock all the locks but you have to figure out the keys to use.' "

"Ask the lid how you can raise it."

"Lid, how can I raise you? It says, 'You have to use your mind, not your muscles. You will have to know when it's time.' "

"Do you hear anything else?"

"I have all the knowledge I need. From now on, it's my responsibility—the box isn't going to help."

"Ask the box where you can find the strength to deal with this situation."

"It says, 'You have to look to the deepest place inside, to your deepest emotions, and you have to use your mind. Using just your mind or just your emotions is not enough. Both are needed.' "

"Ask the box what it is in you that makes you so weak in this situation."

"It says, 'You allow the past to write your present and your future. You let old fears guide your present. Part of you has grown up and yet you still hang onto old fears that aren't even you anymore.' "

"Ask the box to name your fears."

"Box, name my fears. It says, 'Embarrassment, failure in the eyes of others, saying the wrong thing, saying nothing, giving up before seeing something through, having the cost of something be stronger than the gain. . . .' "

"Ask the box how you can overcome these fears."

"By focusing on my strengths, by working on what's already good, by taking the focus off the fears, by giving myself time for healing. . . ."

"Ask the box what happened to your hand."

"Box, what happened to my hand?" asked Dan. I noticed the tears begin to roll down his face, but made no comment. I felt we were at the brink of important revelation, and hoped he could stay with the experience.

"It says, 'It's the only way to make you stop and see how you are not caring for your whole self. It's what you care about the most, but you are not caring for it. Your self needs to be heard by you yourself. It's what happened with your appendix a long time ago. . . .' "

I remembered how in one of our sessions together, Dan had shared with me how, during his early college years, he had almost died of a ruptured appendix. I directed him back to the box.

"Ask the box how you can care for yourself."

"Box, how can I care for myself? It says, 'Be thankful for the gifts you've been given. Stop being self-critical. Let the good shine through. Let the healing happen that's trying to happen.' "

"I know this is painful, Dan, but let's stay with this as long as possible. Ask the box how you can heal your hand."

"It says, 'Listen to all your other pains. Put your needs first and others' needs second. Care for your body first.' "

"Ask the box if there's something wrong with your hand."

"It says, 'You've been tense for so long and clenched for so long that it can't relax. Your shoulders cry out and your back cries out from strain also. You push too hard. You put deadlines over what you know to be healthy for yourself.' "

"Ask the box, then, if it's telling you that your hand is basically fine."

"Box, is my hand fine? It says, 'You've overworked me so much that my muscles are lazy now and need to be worked to bring you back to peace.' "

"So your hand is overworked?"

"It's been overworked and overworked and overworked for years. It's forcing me to hear."

"Dan, what are you going to do about this situation?"

"I have to listen to all my pains. I have to stop working when the pain starts. I need to focus on relaxing the whole body, not just parts. I must not simply wait for a crisis to take time out."

"What spiritual lessons does the hand have to teach you?"

"Everything has to do with everything. When one part of the body cries out, it affects the whole. All things that are buried continue to come up until you heal them and love them and care for them and grow through the pain."

"Dan, your hand will be made whole when you learn to love yourself. Your hand will be made whole when you learn to take better care of yourself, especially by knowing how to relax and when to let go. Your hand will be made whole when you accept yourself in all your strengths and limitations. Your hand will be made whole when you learn to be more gentle with yourself. I invite you now to turn to the

God of healing and to ask that you will be made whole—that you will be healed physically and mentally and emotionally, and that your memories of past hurts will also be healed. When you are ready, open your eyes and we will discuss what we have learned. . . ."

"I reached a deeper level of understanding than words normally provide," said Dan. "I got deep into past hurts as well as present hurts, but it was not just a dredging up of emotions. I felt that the experience was more controlled— perhaps because of the structure your questions offered me. I felt there was a genuine joining of emotion and intellect in what we did together. It was a different form of cognitive awareness, not just a tapping into repressed emotion. I hadn't made the association with my appendix before, but I feel that insight is on target. That was a desperate time and I did feel boxed in then, as I do now. I was almost ready to go into a healing process when the appendicitis struck, but I realize now that I was setting myself all the wrong goals. It took being landed in the hospital to make me reassess my lifestyle and strategies. Perhaps my hand is suffering now because my hands are so important to me. I use them to play the piano, to do my school work . . . I would say I value them more highly than anything else. I have been over-using them and abusing them, but I also see the spiritual and emotional issues involved in my pain."

"What you do with these insights is for you to decide, Dan. You may decide to seek out therapy, or perhaps to do journal work, or perhaps to do imaging on your own. You could tell your hand that the pain is going to go away and that you are going to take care of it. You might want to read Siegel's work on imagery and healing to give you some ideas about what he does. For my part, I suspect that you will be without your wrist guard before very long. Spiritual therapy and physical therapy will set you straight. . . ."

Several months have passed since this session. During this time, Dan has worked with a physical therapist to regain strength in his hand. He has also focused more on the ways in which he feels "driven" and on the other stresses in his life. At the seminary he is trying to pay more attention to his own inner life and academic performance and less to how he compares with his classmates. He now understands that when he allows stress to dominate him, his body is going to protest in one form or another; he sees that he himself holds the keys to his own well-being.

*   *   *

When Kate came to see me, she had already been in recovery for several months and was continuing to make daily progress. From her account of preceding events, it sounded as though she had been through a harrowing experience. A series of neurological imbalances or irregularities had unexpectedly left her dependent on a walker and on the attention of her husband. Although she was only in her early forties, she had been left with the mobility of a geriatric patient and no sense of what the future would hold for her. A visit to a psychologist had affirmed that she was ill rather than neurotic as she had feared; doctors, however, could not agree on a diagnosis. At first they suspected multiple sclerosis, but they eventually narrowed down her symptoms to a vicious viral attack. She had been told that she would eventually recover, but that it would be a long road toward healing. She felt that she was making good progress and that she had faced most of her issues; at the same time, she was curious about the process of image guidance and wondered whether it could shed any further light on her condition.

In our preliminary discussion, I learned that she was the token woman in an engineering firm. Because she was in a supervisory position, she had continually felt that she had to prove herself to her colleagues and to those who reported to her. She pushed hard, taking on extra projects, working long hours of overtime, never taking sick days or vacation time. She began having anxiety attacks, but just as she had decided to "slow down," she began to sense that there was something wrong with her health. At first she did not pay close attention to the problems she had in standing or walking, but the symptoms continued to build until she realized she was totally out of control of whatever was happening to her. She was hospitalized with possible pneumonia, but it was soon clear that her condition defied diagnosis. For two months her health declined so rapidly that she was unable to walk at all; she felt exhausted and lethargic and became acutely distressed at the lack of a diagnosis. Eventually, however, the team of neurologists and internists agreed that the illness, whatever it was, would eventually burn itself out. The best Kate could do was to live with the question "when?" and to contribute to her own recovery by being as active as possible.

I asked Kate if any image had come to her which reflected this experience.

"Its like a cloud," she said. "It doesn't have much substance, not like a smoke-machine cloud. It's characterized by gray-white translucency. It's loose—light in color, with soft edges. It has an enveloping quality and, at times, a sticky feeling. It clings to me rather like a web and I fear it has the power to enmesh me. I've made progress. I feel confident. I feel I can break through it. I'm determined. It had the potential to have power over me but it doesn't presently have power. It doesn't have a restrictive quality. It won't hold me. It feels as though there will be plenty of opportunities to break out of it. It's simply a question of finding the right hole. It has taken me a while to accept the time involved, but I now believe I can will the effects of the cloud to be less

severe. The times when I slip back into worrying are temporary. The stickiness grips for a little while, but this is fleeting.
This cloud is not a threatening image—I can see the summer
sky through it. It has a benign appearance. At first it was like
a thunderstorm cloud, but there is no longer the blackness. I
see improvement all the time. . . ."

As I listened, I was struck by the certainty in Kate's
voice and also by the strength that I heard. She sounded like
someone who had come to understand her own power and
who had learned radical hope even when confronted with
disintegration. There was no note of denial or wishful-
thinking; rather, there was courage and authenticity. Even as
I invited her to relax and to focus on the image of the cloud,
I wondered whether our session would have anything new to
reveal to her.

"Where are you?" I asked.

"I'm half in the cloud and half out of it," said Kate.

"Standing on the ground?"

"No, sitting in the cloud—I'm not in contact with the
ground, but the force of gravity is pulling me down. I'm
happiest when I'm on the ground. I feel enveloped by the
cloud—it's a swirling mass that moves and changes, depend-
ing on how my symptoms change. There are some days when
I feel better than others. There are some days when I feel
better with more to do. I always feel there is something out
there, waiting for me, beyond that cloud. I'm not sure
what. . . . It's as though I still can't see what's lying ahead
because there is something—a brick wall or obstacle?—
perhaps a passageway. . . . I feel there's a transitional ele-
ment in process. . . . I'm willing to take my chances on a
new state of being. . . . I'm not sure what it is, but I'm
excited. . . . Up until last year, I had a boring life. I liked
what I did, but it was overwhelming—punishing in some
ways, gratifying in small ways. I felt no enjoyment in life, but

knew a better balance must be possible. I was searching and the search was ongoing. . . .

"Since my illness, I've been determined to do things for myself and to pursue my own interests, even if this has meant working part-time hours. My family is growing older and I feel the need to spend time with them, not with some client who really doesn't care about me. I have to state my needs so that I remember what they are. I'm still doing a good job—being responsible and ending up with a good product, but there is more balance in my personal life. . . .

"I feel that everything will be fine. The simple decision to work less and not to be burdened gives me time to think of those things I really want to do. I feel free to choose. Money really isn't an issue, but self-worth and satisfaction are. I have a transitional feeling—that I am breaking out of the cloud, but it takes a lot of effort. It's not easy—there are many side issues, but they don't have to influence my decision, whatever it will be. I'm confident. I'm hoping that all my physical and mental effort will bring about change. . . ."

"Ask the cloud why it came to you," I directed.

"So, Cloud, why did you descend on me?" asked Kate. "It was a reaction and an opportunity," she said, almost immediately. "An opportunity to take advantage of a weakened body and a confused mind, an opportunity to overwhelm and obscure some of the issues and physical problems so they couldn't be seen, an opportunity to make me take another path. But the illness was already there—the cloud didn't cause the illness. My emotions were hampered by this physical problem—impaired, perhaps? The cloud was a screening device—a blanket which covered everything over so that I could deal with issues one at a time. It says, 'I came to help you gradually sift through your issues and make you aware of them so that you could pay attention and bring them to resolution, but I was not the cause of your illness.'

Which is a mystery to me," commented Kate. "It feels as though I can beat this disability, however long it takes—a year, perhaps, or even longer. I know that more time is needed for physical healing and to work on those issues that became apparent through the cloud."

"Ask the cloud why you became ill," I instructed.

"Cloud doesn't know. A good guess is stress or environment. There are so many unanswered questions, so much dissatisfaction with the modern world of medicine. Cloud really doesn't have concrete evidence or reasons why I got ill. Sometimes Cloud doesn't address my illness—it simply accepts it and expects me to work on this on my own. Sometimes, when I feel an enveloping sensation, it's when I don't want to work on my illness and get a little lazy. Then Cloud settles around me, but it is not judgmental. It's up to me to break out—I'm the one in control. Cloud is almost a separate entity. It's up to me to find a path out of it, to look for ways to improve my condition. . . ."

"Ask Cloud what you need to do next," I said.

"So, Cloud, what do I do next? How do I keep on improving? It says, 'Well, you can't stop trying. You can't be complacent. It's not easy—it's not fun and there's still the search for what you want to do next, beyond what you're doing now and beyond combining what you're doing now with something else. Talking to people is so important, and interacting with people. . . . Doing buildings and roads is not always the most satisfying goal—you're dealing with inanimate objects, even if others say they're not. You need to deal more with people than with structures. So how to proceed with this? You need to keep working at regaining understanding; you need to keep the momentum going with personal relationships and stop being such a mole. Enjoy the city and the world now, instead of waiting until you retire and are dropping dead' (there's a big work ethic within my family, commented Kate). 'You can do other things that are enjoyable. There's not much enjoyment in the attitude, "How can we keep them from suing us?" What's most important is your emotional state, your happiness. You just went from day to day, from week to week, and the years would go by without you thinking about your emotional state. . . .

" 'What have you accomplished? Plenty, but there are other things to accomplish. You have to take the first step and take a chance. Maybe you need to run away from work and back to school. Maybe you don't have to do anything just now. Let everything become clear to you. . . .' "

"Does this make sense, Kate?"

"In some ways it does, but I feel a sequence has to be followed. I think I know what the sequence is: first I have to recover and think of something to do when I'm ready to do it; then I have to do it. There are so many things I could do that I have to narrow my choices down. There are four or five things which appeal to me, and cutting back my work schedule would give me the time. I'm hesitant about going back to working weekends and evenings; parts of me say there are things I could be doing which are socially relevant—building shelters for the homeless, for example, or helping people who are trying to get off welfare and who need a place to live.

"Status symbols don't interest me so much. As time goes on, I feel the need to explore some options I've discussed with friends—setting up a business, for example. Having ideas makes me feel better—there will be a time when I can do them. These days, I often feel limited, a little frustrated: I don't like being downtown all the time, particularly in rush hour when there's all the messiness of winter. Another cloud sometimes settles on me—a feeling comes over me of slowness; I become angry with myself because I am so dependent. I need to keep myself aware that this is temporary. There may not be 100% recovery, but it will be enough.

I need to stop getting jealous when I hear people making travel plans."

"Is there anything else you want to ask Cloud?"

"I'm not sure I have specific questions for Cloud, but one question which popped into my mind was, 'Will you go away? Or mutate? Or evolve? Will you obscure things, but not beneficially?' I think that if I keep conscious, it will be up to me how Cloud and I interact. Will it sink back into the ground the way it started or will it simply lift? I haven't had any profound spiritual thoughts during this time. Most of my thoughts have been rooted in a selfish attitude. If I end up helping people, will it be for them or for me, to inflate my ego? This whole experience needed to be selfish, because only by thinking about the self could I change my situation. Now it's time to think about my husband and my family—they've all been great and I need time to include them more in my life."

"Ask Cloud how long it is going to be around."

"How long are you going to be around, Cloud? It says, 'That depends on you. If you don't need me anymore, if you aren't dependent on other people. . . . Or maybe I won't go even if you told me to leave. . . . It depends on how long it takes you to reach the stage where you are self-sufficient. Maybe you can break out totally and I will dissipate.' "

"How do you feel, Kate?"

"Satisfied. I've probably know all this all along. It's not just a physical issue but a mental one also. I've learned that there's a lot of prejudice against people with handicaps. I need to make sure I've come to terms with prejudice. The cane doesn't bother me these days—I do have mental capabilities. My goal is to be back to normal; I am therefore hopeful that the cloud will just go away."

"You mentioned that you don't have much of a spiritual focus."

"No. There's not been an obvious change in philosophy. I've not been struck by a TV evangelist and found God. I don't really feel that anyone is watching over me. It's my challenge and I have to work it out."

"Ask Cloud its reaction to this response."

"Cloud doesn't have a strong opinion—it's up to me to find my own happiness in life. However I do it is fine. Cloud is not judgmental and doesn't think there is anything wrong with separating the good from the bad, the reality from the spirit, as long as you have both. They may function in different ways, but reality and spirit act separately and yet influence each other. Cloud has no opinion, which I guess is my opinion. I wonder if Cloud contradicts itself?"

Rather lost by these last words and realizing that our session had been in progress for almost two hours, I asked Kate to thank Cloud for those gifts it had given her. It felt like an appropriate time to bring the session to a close. Out loud, eyes still closed, Kate listed those things for which she was thankful:

"I do feel thankful for the opportunity to see myself differently, for discovering opportunities which I had only partially formulated, for finding the freedom to interact with friends, for feeling less obligated, for accepting myself, for being happy with what I have, for being excited about my future, and for not being so overwhelmed that I cannot see where to go next. And I'm most thankful for being able to recover enough that Cloud isn't a menacing figure, but a benign being which shelters my emotions and makes me take care of my destiny."

There was little to process. Kate's words had spoken for themselves, and her dialogue with Cloud basically revealed what she already knew. She left feeling affirmed and even more confident than when she had come to see me; I, for my part, was left in amazement at the power of the inner world to speak so eloquently to those attuned to its voice. As in Dan's case, Kate's illness had come as teacher and friend—a painful inconvenience, yes, but one that was necessary if the stresses inherent in her lifestyle were no longer to have a stranglehold over her.

Image Guidance and
Serious Conditions

My belief in synchronicity, that is, in meaningful coincidences, was strongly reinforced at a recent conference. During a session on symbolism, the woman sitting next to me stood up and briefly mentioned how, less than a year before, she had been diagnosed as having terminal cancer; it was her use of imagery, she claimed, that had been responsible for her healing. After the session, I asked if she would share more of her story with me. I explained how my own interest in imagery had led me to explore its possible health care applications, and asked if I could use her story as part of my data. We agreed to meet later that night, in my hotel room.

Intrigued, I listened to Diana's story. She began by describing what had been going on in her life in the summer of 1990. Her husband was out of work, her sister was having surgery for the removal of a massive tumor, her daughter was facing open heart surgery and her teenage son was causing havoc with patterns of truancy and drug abuse. In that intensely stressful climate, Diana, then barely forty, began experiencing pain in her right leg. At first she dismissed this as stress-related. Then, when the pain intensified, even after her husband had found a job, she sought out medical help, only to be told she had bursitis. Cortisone and more exercise were ineffective solutions. A new doctor laughed when she cried in reaction to a cortisone shot, telling her that the pain was in her head. For several months after that, she ignored the pain as best as she could. On the day her daughter had open heart surgery, Diana was admitted to a hospital with the diagnosis of rhabdomyosarcoma, a rare form of cancer. She was told her options were massive radiation and chemotherapy or death within the year. The main tumor turned out to be the size of a softball and surgeons removed so much surrounding muscle that they warned her that she would probably never walk again.

As I looked at Diana, it was hard to believe that she had ever been so seriously ill. She walked without even the trace of a limp, and showed no signs of ever having been ravaged by disease. "Well, now I not only walk but dance," said Diana. "Doctors had no medical explanation for my recovery. At first, I came down with infection after infection after I began the chemotherapy—in fact, on two occasions I nearly died. I was put on a new drug which was supposed to stimulate the production of white cells, but it never kicked in. I also got severe radiation burn—so badly that I couldn't sit for six weeks and had to have skin and muscle grafts. That was the only time I had to take time off work for any extended period of time. I was supposed to have twelve treatments of the chemo, but I quit after the fifth treatment—I had thrown up seventeen times in one day and couldn't take anymore. Now I've been cancer-free for a year. I don't claim to be cured because one can only use that word after five years. . . ."

"So how does imagery fit in?" I asked.

"When I was admitted to the hospital, I had a temperature of 104°F. My daughter had just come out of surgery and my son had just run away again. I felt totally out of control. The doctors didn't want me to take Tylenol because they wanted to see where the temp would spike. My sister was with me and she encouraged me to relax. I was used to doing relaxation exercises both at home and at the office and also to using the active imagination, but my body was on fire and I was unable to help myself in any way. My sister got me breathing deeply and then asked me to imagine myself lying on a beach. The warmth I experienced was the sun's warmth, she said. I began to relax and soon felt that I could let go of the fear and anxiety. My sister led me through a guided meditation that had me focusing on building sand castles, on feeling the breeze, on seeing the cool water. She asked me to remember childhood memories—especially things that made me feel happy. Gradually, the temp began to go down.

"After this experience, I asked friends and family if they could write down any happy memories of times we had shared together. It was a wonderful process—gave me many laughs. I was able to concentrate on positive images instead of on all the pain. I also began using a Bernie Siegel tape. It involved going into a garden, but I created my own English garden which became a place of refuge for me, a kind of sanctuary. I also began having some powerful dream experiences. Around the fourth chemo treatment, I had lost my identity and had begun to see myself as a sick person. The way I related to everyone was influenced by my illness. Then I began having dream images of a vast crater. It was much greater than any crater I had ever seen. I thought perhaps it was like the craters one sees on the surface of the moon. In my dreams, I placed a table in the middle of the crater and sat there, on the edge of nothingness, surrounded by this vast space that only God could fill up. My images told me that the space had been created by everything that I had gone through; they invited me to rest in the space. I remember having a very powerful dialogue with these dream images; they began to sustain me and I began to recover. . . ."

I asked Diana if she would be willing to return to her dream images and to see whether the crater had anything more to tell her at this time. I darkened the room, and as she relaxed, I instructed her to focus again on the crater and on all that it contained.

"I see darkness all around and the crater is dark and yet there's a sense of distinction between the darkness and the crater. I can see clearly although it's dark. The crater is not made of mud but of rock and it's immense. It's rugged, not like anything on earth I've experienced. It's round and open, symmetrical, and I can walk around it. It's deeper than I'm tall, and my table is there, not in the center but off to one side. And the scripture that comes to me is, 'I stand knocking and all you have to do is invite me and I will sup with you.' No one's at the table. It's small, old, and somehow it's lighted. But there's a vast emptiness in the cavern. It's almost like the kinds of stretches you see in moon craters. . . ."

"And where are you?" I asked.

"I'm not in the center and also not at the table but near to the side. I can walk toward the edge of the crater and look over so that I can see land all around it which is a vast continuation of the dark rocky surface. It's not been attacked by whatever attacked the surface to form the crater. I'm wondering if the blackness is almost like the blackness that's left from being charred, burned. It's not like ashes, but like wood that's been badly burned. I haven't touched the surface before—I've only walked around it."

"Try touching the surface of the crater," I suggested.

"It's hard, rough. I can't tell if it turns my hand black or not. It's too dark. I can't tell if it was charred at one time or another."

"Ask the crater, 'How did you get black?' " I instructed.

"It says, 'I was created that way. I was always black and

empty and you still want to fill me up and you don't need to fill me up.' "

"Ask the crater why you need to leave it empty."

"Why do I need to leave you empty, crater? It says, 'Because it's not your place to fill me up. That's someone else's job, if I am ever to be filled.' "

"Ask the crater what your job is."

"Crater, what is my job? It says, 'I told you to tell the story, to write the story, and you haven't done it. That's your job. You've tried to tell it in some places but you need to write it. Margaret told you to write it.' "

"But I don't have the energy to write it," protested Diana.

"Start at the beginning," said the crater.

"All the way back to Daddy's suicide attempt—is that what you are saying?"

"That's the beginning," said the crater.

"Am I supposed to take what I've already written and use that?" asked Diana.

"That would be a start," said the crater.

"I was waiting for the computer. . . ."

"That's a good excuse, but you can get the computer whenever you want it."

"It's a dumb time to spend money on a computer with the wedding to pay for. . . ."

"There's never going to be a good time," observed the crater. Just get the computer or do it on a typewriter."

"I'm beginning to feel that the computer is a lame excuse," said Diana. "If it's not the real reason, what is it?"

"That's for you to figure out," said the crater.

"Why won't you tell me?"

"Because you're resisting it."

"I'm afraid of the pain," said Diana.

"I don't think you're afraid of the pain," said the crater. "You know how to work through pain. But you'll surely discover something you don't know."

"But the things I discover are usually life-giving."

"They're always life-giving."

"So what am I afraid of?"

"The unknown. Not being in control."

"I don't really buy that," objected Diana. "Control is no longer an issue. . . ."

"It's always going to be an issue."

"So I'm afraid of losing control? I know how to go with the flow. I've learned to be flexible. I've learned how to let the holy take over when I'm resisting. . . ."

"What are you afraid of, Diana?" I interjected. Until this point, I had remained a silent spectator, listening to her dialogue with the crater, recording what I heard as accurately as possible while monitoring how Diana was bearing up emotionally.

"Maybe there's a fear of something in my childhood," she said. "It's almost as though I feel guilty because my childhood was charmed in relation to my sisters and my brothers. I didn't experience any difficulties until I was in my teen years, but one of my sisters was sexually abused by a cousin from the time she was 8 to when she was 18. Maybe there's a fear that my other younger sisters were also abused. Then there's the discovery of my father's suicide attempt—I discovered this through prayer. I don't want to know more. My sisters considered me to be their mother and I couldn't protect them. I didn't even know what was going on—I was too naive to even imagine what my cousin was up to. How is telling the story of what I've been through going to help? Why do I have to drag up all of that stuff?"

"Because it's all connected," said the crater. "It's not isolated."

"Why should I feel guilty? I was a child. I realize that I'm not to blame for what happened to Jenny, and if it happened to some of the others, it's their story."

"But their story is intimately connected to your story," insisted the crater.

"But I was a child! I can't be held responsible," cried Diana, tears streaming down her face.

"You know this in your head, but you don't know it in your heart," said the crater. "You feel you should have been able to help them. You're no one's savior—not even your own."

"I don't understand what all this has to do with the crater."

"You're afraid. To know your destiny you have to follow fear."

"I'm tired of following fear. It makes me angry. I've followed fear to the depths of this crater and it's agony. I've been crucified. . . ." She continued to speak through her tears, "It's time for joy. I don't want to walk through the pain anymore, and that's why I'm not writing the story. . . ."

"You're afraid of the pain," said the crater.

"I don't want to relive it."

"Don't you see it will be different?" asked the crater. "It's like the road to Emmaus. Jesus could tell the story of his suffering, but there was resurrection and joy. And he was so different they didn't recognize him and you're so different that there won't be any pain in the telling. Just write it. They will listen."

"Who is they?" asked Diana.

"I don't have the answer to that question. The story simply has to be written."

"Will it make a difference to the medical profession?" she asked.

"I want them to be changed," said the crater. "Somehow they need someone to tell them. Your job is to write the story—"

"They're so insensitive," she objected. "And they don't have a clue. They don't have the skills to help people to be healed. . . ."

"That's a generalization and you know it," said the crater. "They're not perfect. You can't expect them to be perfect. O'Connor will read the story."

"Who's O'Connor?" I asked.

"My radiation oncologist. The only doctor I've chosen to maintain a relationship with. He's following my case. He's a wounded healer—he needs to tell his story. . . ."

"That's a pious attitude," said the crater.

"Why do you say 'pious'?" she asked.

"For want of a better word. You think you are so high and mighty that you can decide what other people are supposed to do. Just work on you, O.K.?"

Noting that it was almost 2:00 a.m. and feeling that we had reached a good place to end, I instructed Diana to go to the table in the crater.

"When you hear the knocking," I said, alluding to the scriptural passage she had mentioned earlier, "invite the Holy One in. Ask how you will find joy and strength."

"This is what I hear," she said. "You know your joy is in writing—it gives you strength. It is not something you need strength to do because you become strong through the writing."

"But I need discipline, don't I?"

"You can schedule time for writing like anything else that you value."

"You're right," said Diana. "I have to schedule it and if I'm going to continue to grow, I have to choose to write."

"It's a gift and you must write. It will bring you strength and it will bring you joy."

"I can't imagine being stronger than now—"

"You don't need to be stronger. You need to be renewed—daily, weekly—and writing will renew your strength."

"That reminds me of Martha and that scares me."

"Every time you jump to conclusions you are wrong," said the voice. "Her strength was renewed in her death; your strength will be renewed in your living. She was older. Your story will be told in your living; her story was told in her dying."

"She was a beautiful person, a wounded person, a simple person. . . ."

"You are a beautiful person, a wounded person, a simple person. . . ."

"She was gracious. . . ."

"As you are. . . ." replied the voice.

Diana smiled. "I never thought of Martha as my shadow."

"There's some of Martha in you."

"That's what others see. . . ."

"They see reality. You're special."

"But I'm not supposed to go in the direction of specialness."

"You don't compulsively need to be special—I have chosen you to be my disciple, to go forth and proclaim the good news in the name of the Father and the Son and the Holy Spirit. . . ."

"I can't seem to lose touch with that masculine image of creator," observed Diana. "Have I latched onto that because of my discovery of my father's clay feet?"

"No," said the voice. "You've latched onto that because it's important to be in touch with the feminine and the masculine. There's validity in both."

"Who are you?" she asked.

"I am who I am. I am the God of the present. I am not 'I was' or 'I will be.' I am. Continue to be present to the wound."

"I can see the stars," said Diana, a look of radiance illumining her face. I hadn't seen stars above the crater before. There are stars all around, filling the universe. . . ."

"Diana," I intervened. "The God who strung the stars will fill the crater. The God who strung the stars will fill you with all good things. Thank the Lord who sups with you for his presence and for the good things he has shared with you. Then open your eyes in peace and joy."

Diana's first words on opening her eyes were, "Thank you." I had really done nothing except witness her own rich dialogue with her images, intervening once or twice in the process. I had seen and felt her pain, had heard her story, and had been moved by the grace of the experience. Whatever the future held for Diana, I had no doubt that it would be rich and beautiful and that she would be sustained by the depths of her inner world.

*   *   *

It was almost seven months since Dora's stroke. An active woman in her middle sixties, she had found herself facing severe limitations and an uncertain future. The two minute episode had left her with impaired vision and a useless left arm. Initially, she had been unable to walk, but two months in a hospital rehab unit, followed by intensive physical therapy, had brought about amazing results. As we spoke about the stroke and its implications, I felt some apprehension. Could image work be too painful for her? I asked myself; if we touched on too much darkness, could it, in fact, precipitate another stroke? Was Dora the kind of client who could benefit from image guidance or would she be too resistive to the process? During initial meetings, I always evaluate whether or not image guidance would be an appropriate intervention; in Dora's case, I suspected that the answer was "no."

There was nothing definite on which I could place my suspicions. True, she shared with me that a month after her stroke, she had "fallen apart" so dramatically that she was now seeing a psychologist with a specialty in rehab work; at the same time, however, she had been under his care for six months already and was able to speak about her stroke and its consequences without any obvious distress. Still, I felt uneasy. We continued to chat about her experiences in the hospital, and I tried to get more in touch with my own feelings about working with her.

She focused mostly on the kindness she had received following her stroke—the attention she received in the hospital, the thoughtfulness of neighbors who had taken care of her plants and of her cat, the generosity of friends from work and church. "I don't like being around negativity," she said. "Negativity always makes me feel bad. I like to focus on the positive." As I heard these words, I wondered whether focusing on imagery connected with her stroke would be "negative"; plunging into the darkness of one's pain is not for everyone.

"Dora, I want to remind you that image guidance can take us into painful territory; I *am* concerned about us working together, so we will need to move slowly. If it gets too uncomfortable, all you have to do is open your eyes. What's important is that you let me know how you're feeling as we go along. I don't want to take you back to when you had your stroke—I don't think you're ready for that yet. What would be useful is for you to dialogue with an image of your stroke to find out how you can continue to make progress. What we will do together is find out what your stroke 'looks like' and the kind of personality it has. We're going to treat it as a living being with whom you can hold conversations, not simply as something that happened to you."

"Liz, I don't think I've ever thought about how my stroke looks. I haven't wanted to look at it. The only image I get is of the Blessed Mother. We have a very close relationship—always have, ever since I was born. When I think of her, I feel peaceful. You'll have to help me focus on the stroke."

"We could begin with color. Does it have any color that you are aware of?"

"It's dark—a deep gray, not black. It's like a shadow, but it has no shape. It's simply there. Again, whenever I feel the presence of the shadow, I think of the Blessed Mother. . . ."

"Dora, we'll begin with some relaxation exercises, and then we'll try dialoguing with the shadow. We'll ask it simple questions about how you can help your arm mend and whether there's anything you can do to improve your vision. I'm going to follow your lead. All you have to do is open your eyes when you feel uncomfortable."

I turned off the standard lamp near her chair and moved a table away from her. I looked at the open blinds and half moved toward closing them.

"I usually work in a darkened room—does this seem too bright to you?"

"No—this is fine," said Dora. I made a mental note of how bright the room seemed to me, even without the benefit of electricity. Perhaps her need for light was another indication of her avoidance of the dark side of life. I would have to proceed with caution.

"Dora, sit as comfortably as you can. Take a deep breath and hold it as long as you can; now breathe out, slowly. Breathe in; breathe out. . . . Breathe in strength, peace and hope; breathe out anything that is negative, anything that makes you tense. Breathe in courage and grace;

breathe out any darkness that you might be feeling, any fear or anxiety. I want you to focus on the image of the Blessed Mother; ask her to hold your hand and to give you her strength. Know that she will protect you. When you feel strong enough and safe enough, focus on the image of the shadow—"

I had spoken slowly and clearly, watching Dora intently for any signs of discomfort. At the first mention of "shadow," she had opened her eyes. "All I can see is the Blessed Mother," she said.

"Dora, that's fine. I don't want you to feel that you've let me down or not done what I asked. You're focusing on an image which gives you strength at this time. I don't think you're ready to deal with anything negative. A year from now, when you have made even more progress, you may be ready to try again, but you're still healing. I also think that your dislike of the negative may also work against the process being useful, and we both have to respect that. You have your positive image to give you strength; it seems to me that turning to the Blessed Mother is the most significant image work you can do."

I was relieved at the outcome of our session. From it, I learned to pay more attention to the promptings of intuition. I also learned that judging healing on the basis of chronological time did not make much sense. Though I had assumed that the seven months since Dora's stroke would have left her in a good mental framework to attempt image work, it was clear that it would be many more months—if at all— before we should try again.

Image Guidance and Addictions

I had worked with April for several months in the capacity of spiritual director when she asked me if we could use image guidance to explore her food addiction. Aware of her painful background and of her present vulnerability, I was at first hesitant. In facing the addiction, we would also be confronting, head-on, a childhood filled with incest, physical abuse and shame, and a present that was characterized by uncertainty in terms of work and relationships. And yet there was something in April's wholehearted commitment to inner growth that told me that image guidance might be a useful tool. We scheduled an evening stretch of several hours to allow the space for any healing that needed to be done.

As we prepared for the session, I asked April to reflect on her weight issue and to share with me any memories or associations that came to mind. In this way, I would be able to draw on our conversation during the process itself, and would be more in touch with her own feelings and insights.

"It's hard to speak about my weight in isolation," she said. "It's tied up in my self-image, in my self-worth, in my very identity. It's hard to separate my weight from everything else. As a child, I went from doctor to doctor. In second grade, I was put on thyroid medication and I remember my teacher asking my parents about my weight. I began to feel that my weight was everyone's issue. Everyone talked about it. I couldn't even eat anything without at least one family member saying, 'Should you be eating that?' There's one day I remember in particular. It was in 1986—July. I'll never forget the date—it was July 6th. I'd gone to my grandmother's to take her out to lunch, and I was helping her down the steps, toward the car. She seemed depressed. On the first step, she told me that it was the 40th anniversary of my grandfather's suicide—he had wanted to kill her, too, but she had said no and he had gone off and shot himself. She was still grieving, several husbands later. That was the first I'd heard about how he had died. Then, on the next step, she told me that when I was a child, the family doctor had told my parents that they shouldn't take me out to eat because I was a disgrace to the family. Then, one step further, my grandmother informed me that all the pressure I had received about weight loss when I was a little girl had been because my father wanted me to lose weight, and he pressured my mother to make me do something about it. This came as a total surprise because he'd never said a word to me about my weight—or about anything else, for that matter. I never received compliments or criticism from him. He was always silent. With each step, then, there was a slammer—some revelation that took me by surprise. . . .

"I know I'm jumping around from one idea to the next, but last summer was another significant piece. We had all gotten together in a summer cottage near the beach, and my father came into the kitchen, ignoring me and everyone else. Immediately, I began to wonder what I had done wrong. Then I remembered that that's the way I felt when I was a child. I felt that any time my parents had any problems, it was my fault, because of my weight, and that if they ever got divorced, it would be my fault. . . .

"At different times, I was involved with weight loss problems. I would lose so much weight, then stop, and then regain it all within a matter of months. I realize now that each of the weight gains was associated with the abuse. I think I tried to punish myself for what was happening. One time I remember in particular was in seventh grade. I had done really well on a diet and stayed at that weight until ninth grade, when a new pattern of sexual abuse began. I started gaining it back and continued gaining, all through high school. . . ."

As April herself had pointed out, it was obvious that her weight problem involved complex issues and patterns and that it was intricately connected to the pain of her life. Since our previous meetings had been for the purpose of spiritual direction, it seemed appropriate to begin with prayer. I called upon the presence of the spirit of Truth and comfort, on the God of the brokenhearted, and asked this Presence to accompany her on her journey, to be her strength and protection. Moving directly from prayer into the image process, I invited April to focus on the image of herself in seventh grade and to let me know what she could see.

"Short light brown blondish hair that's parted on the side. Wearing braces on my top row of teeth and wearing a navy blue and white striped knit dress which has a belt around the waist of the same fabric. The dress is a little tight, but not skin tight. Not wearing any make-up or earrings. . . . I have a good complexion—I never got any pimples until college. I can also see a dark pink scar on my face from a surgery I'd had. I'd had surgery the year before, and in seventh grade, to remove some marks on my face. I was always self-conscious about those marks—when I was about six, I fell off a bike (wasn't even mine—I'd taken it) and my face went traveling through the gravel before I lost consciousness. I went through grade school with people telling me I had pencil marks on my face, but I told them it was gravel. . . .

"I see myself, still a chunky roly-poly, even though I'm told I'm not fat. But I still can't wear normal size clothes—my mother has to make all my clothes for me. . . ."

"Ask the little girl how she feels inside," I instructed.

April gave a deep sigh and leaned her head back. I could see that she was moving more deeply into the imagery, more deeply into pain. "Very insecure, very self-conscious. I feel separate, but at the same time I feel connected. I feel separate because I'm different; I feel connected because I have a lot of friends and acquaintances. . . . But I've just remembered that that's the year I lost my two best friends. . . ."

"What happened?" I asked, noting the intensifying pain on April's face.

"I'd known these two since we were three years old. We lived in the same neighborhood, went to nursery school and kindergarten in the same car pool, went to the same grade school. . . . In junior high—I don't know for sure, but I always thought it was because I didn't meet the criteria that they—um—they couldn't ignore my heaviness, my being overweight anymore. . . ."

"So what did they do?"

"They stopped being my friends. We didn't do things together anymore. I didn't have boyfriends like they did—I had friends who happened to be boys, but it was not the same. . . ."

Fearing that the sadness was going to overwhelm her, I asked April to try to focus on the image of someone who was a real friend at that time in her life.

"Her name is Laurie—it's the name I call my inner child, that is, the little girl within me."

"What was so special about her?"

"Well, I was going to say that she liked me for who I was, not for what I looked like, but I'm not sure that's true. She liked my brother, so perhaps she only hung around with me because of him. Maybe she didn't like me as much as I thought she did. . . ."

"Ask Laurie what she liked about you, April," I said, wanting her to focus on something positive.

"I can't hear anything—just a mumble-jumble. Why is it so hard to hear?" The tears beaded on her lashes and began to spill down her cheeks.

"What would you like her to say to you?"

"That I'm a good friend," said April, wiping her eyes.

"Do you think she would say that to you?"

"Yes," she said, through her tears. "But I see myself as so many different things. I see myself keeping busy, always trying to avoid something. . . ."

"If this feels right, ask the seventh grade April what she is trying to avoid."

"April, what is it you are trying to avoid?" asked April. "What do you keep running from?"

Yawning and shivering simultaneously, April mumbled something, but I couldn't make out all the words. I sensed that she was trying to block out what she was hearing.

"What is she anxious about?" I asked.

"I'm not sure," said April.

"Ask her how she managed to lose weight in seventh grade. What gave her the strength to do it?"

"Seventh grader," said April, "what made you decide that you were going to stick to this diet, that you were going to lose weight? She says, 'I guess that I knew I could do it. I didn't want to be called "fatty," and I didn't want all the attention that being overweight had brought me. I thought that if I lost weight, maybe they'd leave me alone. I could just disappear. But it didn't work. . . .' "

"Why didn't it work, April?" I asked.

"Because they tried to tell me something that I knew wasn't true—they tried to tell me I looked fine. It bothered me for a bunch of different reasons. I didn't like all the attention. They still saw only 'that pretty little face' and nothing else. . . ."

"As you look back on the seventh grader, April, does she look fine to you?"

"No—oh, no. She's kind of ugly. Homely. She still looks fat to me."

"And yet she lost all that weight—how much weight does she have to lose to look thin, April?"

"I don't know," she said. "Another 30 pounds, 40 pounds, 50 pounds—"

"So she would be roughly 110 pounds in weight and 5'8" tall—how would she look then?" I asked, struck by April's inability to see herself as thin.

"I still see the chubby cheeks. . . ."

"Even at 110 pounds?"

"Yes."

"How much weight does she have to lose to get rid of the chubby cheeks?"

"I think they're there to stay."

"So no matter how much weight you lose, you'll always have chubby cheeks?"

"Yes," said April, looking more and more overwhelmed by despair.

"Ask your friend Laurie what she thinks about this," I instructed, knowing that I needed to move her to a more positive place. April scratched her head and fidgeted. "I'm feeling resistance," she said.

"That's because you don't want to hear what she has to say," I said. "I'm going to be Laurie and you can be April. Ask Laurie what she thinks and I'll answer for her."

"Laurie, if I keep on losing all the weight I want to lose, what d'you think?" asked April.

"I think your chubby cheeks will go, and your health

will go and you'll stop laughing and you'll melt away and I won't have a friend," I replied, answering for Laurie. The words had come to me spontaneously, and though they came from my mouth and were spoken in my voice, I felt as though they had been significant.

April scratched her head again and looked agitated. "I don't want to lose my laughter. That's one of the things I did want to hear her mention; it's one of the things I want to hear she liked about me. . . ."

"So your laughter is important to you?" I asked. "Is it more important than chubby cheeks?"

"I'd like to think so. It's what got me through the hell I lived with—one of my escapes—"

"April, I think we've reached some important truths here. You are a person of laughter. Say to yourself, out loud, 'I am a person who laughs. I am a person who can help others laugh.' " After April had repeated these words out loud, I instructed her to say, "I can work on my outside, if my inside is laughing."

She smiled a little as she repeated these affirmations, and I had a sense that the deep sadness was lifting a little. "Ask God for the gift of laughter," I said. "Ask God to help you believe that you can work on your outside, if your inside is laughing. Then, when you feel strong, open your eyes."

When we processed the session, I observed how April's negative attitude toward herself seemed to feed the addictive process. April agreed. "If nothing I do can take away the weight I want to lose, then this keeps me in the addictive process because there's no point trying. I really resisted hearing any positive comments—at one point, when you wanted me to listen to Laurie I think, I began to feel really cold and began shaking. I felt really overwhelmed—I wanted to resist, and at the same time I didn't want to. It was as though air stuck in my throat and I wanted to say something but couldn't. Remembering the laughter was a turning point, though. It made me feel hopeful."

I suggested that April should continue to work with self-affirmations and that she should try to find ways of celebrating the part of her that still delighted in laughter. We both agreed that the key to her weight management would be learning to see herself more positively.

*   *   *

Nancy had also been seeing me for spiritual direction when a food addiction surfaced as a block in her spiritual life. She was not overweight by any means and so I was surprised when the food issue came up. Always impeccably dressed and seemingly self-confident, she was in touch with her own inner world and served as a guide to others. However, beneath the surface there was an ongoing struggle with the desire to cram food into the empty places in her life and then with the subsequent feelings of guilt. Nancy visualized her eating disorder as an impenetrable block.

"Ask the block where it came from," I instructed.

"It says my childhood, but I think I'm the one giving the answer."

"Let's test it anyway," I said, knowing full well that people in the imagery process often express a concern as to where their data are coming from. "Ask the block what it means by your childhood."

"Again, I'm not sure if I'm saying this or if it's coming to me from somewhere else. I think I'm on the right track, but we were just talking about childhood so I wondered whether I am hearing what I was saying before. The block reminds me that I was always different and alone and that I never found the love I needed, and so I kind of put up this block so I could stay apart. I was afraid and the block was like a protection. No one could enter into my world; I was safe and yet I was lonely. But the safety was stronger than the loneliness. I could be inside the block and find comfort in food."

"So the block was a way of shutting people out and letting food in?"

"Yes."

"How did you shut people out?"

"By being very shy, by not being outgoing. I was a friendly child—I talked to people and yet I was afraid of them."

"What were you afraid of?"

"That I couldn't meet their standards. Kids can be mean and I was afraid that if I couldn't be one of them, they would shut me out, so I shut myself out before it happened. I always felt very alone and had to companion myself and look within myself for what I needed instead of getting it from others. I still do this to this day—with my husband. It's still a lonely journey."

"You've said before you've had a hard time with your emotions—do you see a connection?"

"I'm just becoming aware of anger and loneliness. Now I see it's loneliness and sadness. Those feelings hurt."

"What would make you feel better?"

"Having a better relationship with my husband. He's dealing with a lot of issues with his parents right now and needs to work things out. I feel he shuts me out and would like him to accept me. Then there's the pastor—that also involved an issue with hard feelings. . . ."

"What do you do when you feel shut out?" I asked, continuing to address Nancy rather than her image.

"I become withdrawn and eat. Tom's parents domineered him and I would go into my own little shell. Now he needs me to comfort him with this family issue but I need the comfort myself."

"Where can you get it from?"

"I don't know. I feel alone. God's out there but I don't

feel he loves me unconditionally. I don't feel peace and I know that in spite of difficulties, I should be able to feel peace. I get very upset when I eat sugar or candy. I'm in a real process of exercising and do positive thinking, but then I feel the loneliness and eat. This brings negativity and I get angry and have this nagging feeling that I blew it. There's a scripture quote—in Romans, I think—something about not letting food ruin the person for whom Christ died. I know food has become a spiritual issue, that it stands in the way of my relationship with God. I'm out of control."

"Ask the block what you need to do to unblock your path to God," I said.

"It's not talking to me. It doesn't have a voice—it's so hard."

"Nancy, see yourself chipping at the block—tell me what you can see and hear."

"It's funny—the block is hollow inside. I was chiseling away at it and broke through in a second. It's hollow, not solid," said Nancy, seemingly overcome with amazement.

"How does this make you feel?"

"It's a relief—it seemed as if it was hopeless. I felt I could never empty that block, but now it seems as though I've got an answer."

"Ask the block why it was so easy for you to break it."

"It's saying that it never meant me to be so upset with it. Really, it's like a little boulder or a stone, but I made it into a mountain. I'm not seeing the whole picture—if I look at the whole picture, it won't be so big. I'm too close to it."

"So it's your perception of the block which makes it worse than it is?"

"Yes—it's really hollow inside. I felt hopeless because I thought I would never be able to conquer it."

"So what is keeping you from experiencing God's love?"

"It seems that I have to step back and live in the now. I have a vision of meadows, trees, sun and flowers. I need to see God's love in that meadow and to absorb it; I need to breathe in the love he had in creating these things. I can't go and walk in the meadow right now—I'm always looking beyond, ahead. I have to let go and step back. I have to let go. . . ."

"Of what?"

"Of resentment, especially toward my in-laws, of anger, of fear. The block says I need to loosen, I have to let go. Somehow I'm hanging on."

"Ask the block why you are so afraid of letting go."

"I think—and I don't know if it's me saying this, or the block—that everything has to be in black and white for me. By hanging onto the block, I've found security. I'm afraid to let go."

"What else do you need to do?"

"I need to relax. I think of how busy I am. It's funny that I'm saying that. Yesterday a very strong feeling came over me as I was walking. It told me that I need to get away from my busyness at this time. I need time to do things for myself—I've always been doing things for others. Trying to fit in time for me is almost too stressful. I need to pray about this, so that I'll know what I'm meant to be doing—or not doing. The block tells me that the meadow is the place where I'll be free to walk with God."

"Ask the block if it has any wisdom to share with you at this time."

Nancy smiled. "I say 'he'—it's more of an it—he's saying, 'Go for it, Nancy—you know, do what you want to do. Even simple little things around the house. You don't have little kids to keep you back. . . .' The block tells me that I can find God, but I just have to take quiet time—not just one hour in the morning, but walking outside in the spring and watching the trees blossom, finding God in nature. . . . I'm always looking for answers. I need to let go of analyzing. I need to live as a simple child. I'm too much into 'why'—I have to let go. . . ."

"Does the block have any wisdom to share about what you should do when Tom shuts you out?"

"I'm not sure I'm getting this from the block—we need to do a lot of work, Tom and I. In my busyness, in doing so much, in the hurt I felt as a child and with his own parents, I went into my own little world. I need to open up that world, but I don't exactly know how."

"Ask the block what you need to do when feelings of loneliness come over you and you want to eat."

"I'm not getting an answer to that. I need to chisel away the whole block, but I don't know how. Right now I can see that the block is hollow—I need to break the whole thing, to chisel it all away. I need to make it all little stones and gravel."

"Nancy, ask God to give you the strength to chisel away at the block. Thank God for any revelations you have received and, when you are ready, open your eyes."

We returned to the image of the block in several sessions following this initial work. The image represented blockage in prayer and also blockage of emotions; the food addiction, it turned out, was only a symptom of other problems which were more deep-seated. Though through her rigorous discipline, Nancy had managed to keep to her ideal weight, the underlying causes of her addiction were still present, especially loneliness and anger. These causes, in turn, were preventing Nancy from living as fully and as freely as she wished. By taking the block to prayer, by thinking about her relationships, and by monitoring the occasions which she typically turned to sugar for comfort, Nancy was able to understand different facets of her situation. Presently, she is moving toward the idea of ritualizing her desire to surrender to God and to reject all that the block stands for in the presence of a few chosen friends. Such a ritual would empower her to leave the addictive process behind her and to feel the ongoing support of those present.

"Image Guidance and My Diabetes" by Judith-Rae Ross

In December, 1978, I noticed that my mouth sometimes felt "cottony." During the winter I was thirsty and I would urinate heavily. But this was the year of the great blizzard and lots of people had the same symptoms, so I didn't pay much attention. I was tired, but to get to the class I taught at Northeastern I was walking eighteen miles a week, through snow, ice and wind. And that could tire anybody.

In June of 1979, I went for my yearly physical. Everything was in order, pending the blood work. My doctor's last words to me were, "I find you a generally healthy young woman." But the nurse nodded when I asked her if there was any sugar in my urine and told me to go easy on sugar.

When I called the doctor a few days later to get the blood work results, he had one question, "Is there diabetes in your family?" I answered "yes, my father," then asked what the blood sugar was. He answered, "371, but you probably won't understand what that means." I did. I asked him if I was diabetic, and he sighed as he said, "based on this blood sugar, yes."

Looking back, I probably had an onset of symptoms in December or January. Fortunately, the walking must have burned blood sugars.

My father was diabetic, so the disease was no stranger. But knowing my father was diabetic and taking insulin, and being a diabetic, were two different things. I thought living without desserts and candy was all there was to it. I wasn't ready for exchange diets, urine tests, Diabenese and feeling weak and nauseous all the time. I wasn't ready for the luncheon when one of the guests at the table kept pestering me to try something sweet until I had to inform her that I was diabetic.

By early August, 1979, I was hospitalized, the diabetes out of control and pains up and down my abdomen. That's when they found out I wasn't type II diabetic. I was insulin dependent, and by now sorely in need of insulin. In fact, nine hours after my first shot I had my first reaction. It was to be a precursor of what was to come.

I left the hospital two weeks later, able to inject insulin anywhere I could reach. By the time I got to the pharmacy to fill my insulin and syringe prescription, I was having a reaction. Our pharmacist poured me a glass of orange juice on the spot.

It didn't take too long to discover I was an insulin dependent, but brittle diabetic. No regime I was ever on was fully able to control the highs and lows. My diet was shifted constantly. I have been on 1300 calorie regimes and 2500 calorie regimes. I have been, and am currently, on a largely fat-free, high fiber regime. I have been on the fat lover's diet, and the no fiber diet. One doctor said it was all right to eat sweets, just take more insulin.

I have used NPH, Lente, Ultra Lente, Regular, Humulins, 70/30 combinations, and now Velosulin. I was on the pump from 1982 to 1985 and am currently on the pump.

But in 1982, my glyco-hemoglobin was over 22 and today it usually stays at ten or below. I largely follow my diet, work with a sugar support team and have developed a vocabulary for dealing with my diabetes. I can communicate concerns and suggestions. I can give my support team the data they need to help me make judgments and alterations in the managements.

Most importantly, I'm no longer in conflict with myself.

Much of the credit goes to image guidance. Liz Vanek and I talked about trying the process in March of 1991. I had just switched physicians and was following a rigorous diet and regime. It was working but I was having constant insulin reactions. I had even been questioned about whether I would consider a transplant.

I was tired and feeling at loose ends. Nothing seemed to work right and I was weak from daily insulin reactions. My nerves were frayed. "Why not try image guidance?" I thought. "It can't hurt anything anymore than it's hurt already."

It didn't take me long to relax, thanks to my Lamaze training. And it felt wonderful just to have the cares of the day fall away. I felt free to talk with my diabetes, to find out why things were going the way they were.

The state of relaxation is a state free from stress, free from right and wrong. It's a state in which you can communicate with your concerns in a non-threatening environment.

I found it a state where I was in complete command. I could call upon my diabetes and listen to what it had to say. But if I wished, I could leave the diabetes and engage in relaxation at any time. I felt secure and in charge, doing something about the disease that had so dominated my life since 1979.

When Liz asked me to visualize my diabetes, I was surprised at what I saw. My diabetes was a purplish brown oblong blob with a lead crystal-like top. It moved ponderously, almost like a large whale. It was at least two or three feet tall.

I wasn't scared by the "blob" as Liz and I called it. In fact, I was glad that my diabetes now had a form that I could see. This was less scary than the enemy I couldn't see.

Liz asked me if I would ask my diabetes what it wanted. I asked, then got the surprise of my life when the "blob" began to talk a blue streak. It was as if my diabetes had been waiting to talk to me, waiting to come closer.

My diabetes had an agenda. It wanted me to relax. It explained to me that I was too tense and that made it difficult for it to live peacefully inside me. Somehow, the insulin would flow more readily if I would slow down. It also wanted more water. Water, for some reason, made it float in that space inside of me.

That imaging session lasted roughly 40 minutes. Once I came out of it, I realized that I had an insulin reaction that had actually been retarded by the imaging sessions. But regardless of the reaction, I felt wonderful.

My diabetes had become real. It had a shape, a form, a color. Instead of battling an invisible enemy, there was an entity that I could talk to and find out what it wanted. Until I began doing image work, the only thing I could do was follow doctor's orders. If my sugars jumped or if I gained weight, I assumed that something had gone wrong. Now I could ascertain what the diabetes needed beyond just following a particular regime. I wasn't helpless. I could take an active role in working with my diabetes. Frankly, I felt empowered.

This isn't to say that everything became better instantly. I still had reactions, some of them serious. There was still stress in my life. But, I had the means of at least seeing my diabetes and talking with it.

Sometimes my diabetes had very explicit suggestions. I was using a blood glucose monitor that was still in the process of being developed. It was flawlessly accurate and didn't need strips.

But there was a downside. The monitor needed constant calibration. In place of test strips the monitor used two solutions and these were always running out. Supplies for this monitor were not readily available.

Furthermore, it didn't come with a case. I was wrapping it in a washcloth, then pinning it with safety pins. It needed a new cartridge supposedly every six weeks. In reality, I was changing the cartridge every four weeks.

Changing the cartridge required sliding the cartridge into place at two points at once. And purchasing cartridges wasn't cheap.

I was always wondering about whether or not I would be able to successfully complete a test with the machine when I needed to test. While personnel at the medical supply house I had used for my former monitor swore they would carry supplies for this monitor, they never quite got them on a regular basis. Test time had become stressful. Even when the monitor was ready, working with two solutions was both tiresome and cumbersome.

But monitors are expensive and I had acquired this one free from the company. I had also become friendly with the diabetic educator at one of the Chicago hospitals that was doing the study on this monitor and she often furnished me with supplies. I didn't want to hurt her feelings. Then supplies grew even harder to get and I was spending an inordinate amount of time on the phone searching for solutions and cartridges.

Liz saw me struggle with the monitor on a day before one of my sessions. After working with it five minutes, it refused to test my glucose. So we asked the diabetes about it.

The blob was adamant. The monitor had to go. It just wouldn't test when I needed to test, supplies were difficult to find, and it was bulky to carry. The monitor had become a stress point.

I called up a medical supply house recommended to me by another diabetic educator and ordered a One Touch II.

Admittedly, I felt like a turncoat when I looked at the new monitor. But after seeing it work, I knew my diabetes was right. Life became much easier. The diabetic educator who got me the previous monitor understood perfectly. "You're not married to the monitor," she said.

Shortly afterward, the monitor I had been using was recalled by the manufacturer.

The summer of 1991 I went on the insulin pump and image guidance helped me through some difficult times, ultimately making it possible for me to come to grips with my diabetes.

I expected life to go much more smoothly once I was hooked up to the insulin pump. Life is full of surprises. The first pump jammed after five days and had to be returned to the manufacturer. The second pump jammed within a week.

With the third pump we found my stomach would not conduct insulin into my bloodstream. I ran sugars over 600. Finally, we decided to attach the pump tubing in my legs and this brought the sugars down.

Then came the reactions. The usual sliding scale for insulin just didn't seem to work for me. The results were daily insulin reactions. I was always hungry, yet I was gaining weight. When I started becoming very irregular, my calories were increased but all fibers were omitted. Mealtimes were miserable without salads, berries, raw vegetables, whole grain breads and cereals, or fruits with their skins.

All of this came to a head in August, 1991, when it was decided I needed a lower GI. The preparation consisted of a liquid diet for 48 hours, laxatives which made me ill, and finally a Fleet enema. Worse yet, during the test the line came out on me and I was covered with barium. It took an additional two days to recover from the test. To add to the embarrassment, I had lost control of my bowels.

Life had gone from one crisis to another. No matter what I did the diabetes had become worse and my days were filled with blood sugar tests and each meal had become a battle. It was at this point that Liz returned from her vacation, expecting to find me in good spirits and ready to resume guidance work with her.

I was ready to resume image work but was very depressed. Nonetheless, I got into a relaxed state and began to ask the diabetes why things were the way they were.

We talked to the diabetes but the diabetes also asked me how I was feeling. In that relaxed state I was able to give vent to my despair and the fear that life would bring just more of the same.

Then something very important happened. I told the diabetes that I was angry I had gotten the disease. "What had I done to you?" I asked. It was as if a scab had been lifted and the pocket of steam underneath it allowed to escape.

Liz and I terminated the relaxed state. Finally, I was agitated with my discoveries and had started to cry. But once I realized that I was hurt and angry, something ugly was released and I could move beyond it.

In an hour-long session in early September I did just that.

I had asked my diabetes what was troubling it. The answers surprised me. First of all, the diabetes told me that it was mad. I was so busy working with the pump that in some way I had neglected it. In truth, life had become a series of blood sugars rather than the blood sugar becoming a way of working with the disease.

The diabetes didn't like the way I referred to it. Early on I began calling my diabetes the "wee hoary beastie." In time, this got shortened to "the beast." The disease didn't like being called a beast. And I realized as I listened to it that by calling it "the beast" I was saying that I hated it. I was in conflict with myself, a stress-producing situation to say the least.

If I could think of my diabetes in a less negative light then I could work with it, rather than against it. I also discovered that while I could visualize the diabetes as a separate entity, it was really a part of me. I was hating a part of myself.

I promised the diabetes that I wouldn't call it a beast anymore and that I would try to love it. I asked it if it had a name. "I'm Elmo Elijah," the diabetes answered. Interestingly, my maiden name is Elias. Since then, I think of my diabetes with a name.

Liz asked me if I could hug my diabetes. It surprised me but I could. The hatred melted away with much of the stress.

That session became a starting point for a new way of thinking for me. I was no longer set against myself, though standard diabetic vocabulary reinforces the conflict.

Medical personnel often ask the diabetic how his or her control is doing, as if there is a part of the diabetic that is evil and must constantly be controlled. I once had a doctor ask me if I was "behaving myself." It's hard thinking of always controlling a part of yourself without thinking there is something bad inside.

After that session I developed a new way of looking at my diabetes and seeing to its needs. I don't control it. I *accommodate* it. This I do by eating a diet that both of us enjoy. Getting exercise on a regular basis, and rest when I need it. If a sugar is high or low I watch to see if the insulin regime needs changing. I ask myself what is wrong, what needs correcting, rather than assuming I did something wrong. I'm not turned in against myself anymore.

I've come to see that basically my diabetes is a part of me and that to hate it is to hate a part of myself. That has gotten me beyond the anger and a lot of the pain.

Once I relaxed, other matters fell into place. At the request of my pump nurse-practitioner, I began working with a dietician who also works with that nurse-practitioner. It turned out I needed a very large amount of fiber. With that my appetite shrank, my cholesterol count lowered, and regularity returned.

Through MiniMed, the company that manufactures the pump, we learned that my basal rates required U40 strength insulin. I now dilute my insulin to U40 strength every morning when I change the tubing. While it takes a few minutes longer, I'm getting better sugars.

At some point, I began viewing the diabetes as a challenge, not an adversary. With that, my self-esteem improved and I am better able to work with the medical professionals that I see on a regular basis. My husband and I attend a support group and, when they occur, conferences on diabetes. All of this makes me feel much less alone. There are people to share my feelings with.

Later imaging sessions found my diabetes getting philosophical. On one occasion it told me that I'm too busy living for the future. It suggested enjoying each moment for what it is.

In another session it suggested getting more exercise. While exercising one day, it explained to me that the movement helped get the insulin into my cells and that burned more sugar. When I repeated this image to my general practitioner, he noted that insulin does two things: It metabolizes sugar while it sensitizes the cells' receptors so they can use the insulin. "It's an interesting image," he said with a smile.

I've also discovered that exercise helps me relax. It gets

the stress out. So I make the time to exercise each day. My insulin requirement has gone down, and so has my weight.

Interestingly enough, the image of my diabetes has changed. Its body is smaller and more purple, with black lines defining each of the sides. The blob is shaped more like a diamond than an oblong mass, and it is firmer than it had been. It's friendlier and smiling. The top of my diabetes has bright yellow and glittering designs on it. It's easier to live with this entity inside me.

By seeing diabetes as something to be accommodated rather than controlled, I've found day-to-day living has improved dramatically. I've lost the guilt that used to be there whenever my blood sugar got too high or too low.

Yes, there are still times when my sugars fluctuate. There are times when something does go wrong with the pump tubing and I don't get my full insulin dose. And yes, there are times when I miscalculate my dietary needs. But the stress is largely gone and through image work I can visualize my diabetes whenever I need to get insight into what's going on. Imaging is a powerful tool.

Perhaps the greatest gift imaging has given me is a new perception of time. By enjoying and working on the current moment I'm making it possible to enjoy a better future. During the summer of 1991 there were times I wondered how long I would live. Now I feel that if I take care of myself it's only a matter of time before more effective treatments are discovered and, ultimately, a cure. There will be a time when the summer of 1991 will be just a bad memory.

What did image guidance do for me? It took my fears, gave them shape, and made it possible to face them. Image guidance gave me a way to communicate and learn from the diabetes. It gave me the means to discover my true feelings about the disease and to work through all the anger and hurt. Finally, it showed me that my attitude was making it difficult to come to grips with the disease. I accepted the diabetes and learned that it was a part of me. Once I learned to love it as a part of myself, then much of the stress melted away. Through image guidance, I found a way to live with the diabetes without setting myself against myself.

Now I have the means of understanding my diabetes and working with it. It has become a challenge, not a curse. Even the image of the diabetes has become friendlier since I worked with it through image guidance.

The best part is that my focus has shifted in the last year. Instead of worrying about whether or not I can eat something without going to the emergency ward, I am planning ways to do things that previously seemed almost impossible.

I walk for longer distances. All I have to do is remember to take my key, glucose tablets, and some money. I can eat different types of foods as long as I stay away from sugars and too many fats. Pastas don't seem to bother my diabetes at all as long as I avoid too much cheese.

One of these days there will be a cure and Elmo Elijah will have earned a rest. Thanks to insights I got from image guidance work, I think I'll be there to see it.

Image Guidance and Other Applications

To come up with a category to fit every possible application of image guidance is impossible. Each time I work with a client, I discover new possibilities; the limits, it seems, are endless. Only in the last couple of weeks I have learned how to use image guidance to help clients with low self-esteem. In our work, we have practiced repeating positive affirmations about appearance, abilities and personality, have returned to childhood events to confront people who were abusive, and have confronted adversaries in the present tense who may have violated boundaries. We have also explored possible career changes through the use of imagery, and have learned how to deal with family conflicts through creative solutions rather than discord. The case studies presented in this chapter represent isolated sessions rather than long term work; each demonstrates the incredible flexibility of the process.

My first contact with Carmen was the message she left on my answering machine; she had left her name and number, stating that she wanted to experiment with image guidance as a way of preparing for childbirth. Intrigued, I returned her call, wondering what she had in mind. In our discussion, I learned that she had already done some image work, but that this involved using pre-fabricated images she had found in a book. One suggestion, for example, was to condition the body not to fight contractions by focusing on the image of an opening flower; as the flower opened, so the woman in labor would surrender to the oncoming contraction and would, in fact, even welcome it. While this had seemed like a useful strategy, Carmen felt that it did not go far enough in preparing her for the advent of her first child. I said that what I could offer would be the opportunity to "tailor-make" the images to her own experience; I also admitted that I had never worked with pregnancy as a focus, but that, so far, image guidance had proved to be highly flexible in every situation in which I had used it. She said that she was interested in scheduling one session, but that what she was really looking for were techniques to take home with her.

When Carmen arrived for her session, I was surprised to find that she was about my age. After fifteen years of marriage, she was about to have her first child. Immediately, I understood her nervousness. She explained that while she had always wanted a family, and while she had been working with fertility specialists, she had nevertheless been caught off-guard by the fact that she was actually pregnant. Even now, barely two months away from her due date, she had difficulty facing the fact that she was indeed going to have a child. She mentioned that the reality had only begun to sink in when she started quilting a comforter.

As we talked, I realized that it was not so much motherhood that frightened her as the actual delivery. Friends had shared horror stories of their own experiences and she remembered only too well the experience of a miscarriage some fourteen years earlier. Apparently, she had been so distraught that she had sworn at all the nurses and had even threatened to walk out of the emergency room. She was not only concerned about the "pain factor," but also wondered whether she would again humiliate herself by fighting her caregivers. My task, then, was to help her develop coping skills for the actual labor/delivery so that she could relax.

I invited Carmen to breathe in confidence, strength and peace and to breathe out fear, anxiety and tension. Then I asked her to focus on the image of her child (she already knew that she was going to have a boy) and to describe what she could see.

"I can see . . . his hair and it's very soft and fine. . . . I can see his eyes starting to open. . . . I can see his hands stretching upward and his feet in the air . . . and I can see myself holding him, wrapping him against me in my robe and he feels warm and peaceful and it feels right."

"How do you feel, Carmen?"

"I feel happy and anxious and excited . . . and all kinds of feelings of being excited and being afraid and hopeful. I feel like . . . I feel like . . . that I have said that I'm going to die."

Though Carmen looked peaceful, I was concerned about what these words could signify. There was the possibility that her nervousness stemmed from the fear of dying in childbirth. She had said nothing prior to this to indicate that this was a preoccupation of hers, but I needed to know precisely what she meant before we could continue.

"What does this mean, Carmen?"

"I feel like . . . that when I look at him, I know that life goes on. I guess my saying 'yes' to his life is saying 'yes' to my death."

"Your death how?" I asked.

"I guess that without having a child, every time I look at everything that is born and dies, I feel separate or detached. Looking at the image of my own child in my arms makes me feel like I'm part of the process of being born and dying."

"So this is not frightening to you, but rather is a feeling of acceptance?"

"Yes—it's more a feeling of acceptance. I feel a stronger connection to life. I am a part of what I see around me."

"When you see yourself holding the child, does the process seem worth it?"

"Um . . . yeah . . . it does. I guess that when I look at myself going through the process of labor, I see myself accepting help from other people. I see myself accepting my own neediness, though I always have a hard time being weak. I ask for what I need, so people can help me. They can accept my vulnerability and helplessness, so I can be humble. I see myself letting myself be vulnerable without humiliation."

"So part of yourself is being born with the child?" I asked, captivated by her openness and willingness to grow.

"Yes—I feel that whenever I can let this happen, I have more to give the child that's coming. If I recognize my neediness, I can recognize his neediness, but if I deny my neediness, I will deny his, too."

"So in giving birth, you are learning how to be a mother. . . . Carmen, ask the child what it was like being born."

"He said that he wanted to stay because it was familiar and warm and easy and comfortable, but there was a force greater than he that sort of called him to come out, and he was resistant yet curious and afraid, yet he felt compelled to follow that force that was calling to him. And there was the fear of the unknown, of how long it would take, of what would be there. And there was the excitement and fear of the unknown. And he wondered who would take care of him and who would keep him warm and who would protect him. And he was filled with fear, anxiety and hope. . . ."

"Ask the child how you could be of help to him as he is being born. What could make his journey easier?"

"He says . . ." Carmen began to laugh. "The vision I get in my mind is the scene in "Star Wars" where Obi-Wan Kenobi dies and Luke Skywalker is in a space ship, speeding down a canal, fighting—it reminds me of the birth canal. Obi-Wan says, 'Let go, Luke. Let the force be with you.' I guess that's what he's saying to me. 'Let go. The Force is with you.' He tells me to let my body relax. Not to fight my body but to let it do what it knows how to do and he says to trust the process and to let go. . . ."

"What do you understand by that, Carmen?"

"Well, I need not try to change the course of what's happening by thinking so much, but instead I need to let my body govern. I need to trust the moment, not worry. I shouldn't worry about labor escalating in the next five to ten minutes, but should stay in the moment."

"Is that something you can do?"

"Hmm. God. . . . I don't know. You know, it's easy for me to—for my mind to believe it, but it is another thing for it to penetrate my being or for me not to stiffen up and become rigid. Somehow, in life—not only in labor—I tend to brace myself for what will happen. I have this false idea that if I brace myself, it will be less painful. But it's not."

"Ask the child for advice," I said, realizing that her fear of labor was still very real. "He has made it through the process. Perhaps he has advice which could help you."

"He says that I should talk about how I'm feeling to the people around me who are trained to help me, and I can keep talking about how I'm feeling right now, listening to their guidance with an open mind, giving their guidance a chance to work before I panic and say I can't stand it. And if I become angry, I should use my anger to empower me rather than to shut people away. I can turn my anger into my strength. I can look forward to the first meeting of my child, myself and my husband. I can think of the joy after fifteen years of a long road which has brought us to the place we've come to now. Fifteen years of struggling and growing that have brought us past the illusion of love into what real love is, so that we can now meet the child who is a part of both of us, knowing that we have something of value to offer him because of the inner work we have done."

"Do you trust this advice?"

"Yeah, I do."

"How does it make you feel?"

"It makes me feel stronger. It makes me feel a willingness and a feeling of surrender."

"You seem peaceful."

"Yes. It makes me feel as if I don't need to struggle with myself and that peace will come as I befriend the whole experience—what my body's doing, the vulnerability, my own neediness. The fight will be over. There won't be this enemy inside of me."

"Where is the enemy now?" I asked, realizing that she was not speaking about the child, but about the voice of negativity.

"The enemy now is a voice that in my head tells me that what I believe in and what my child tells me aren't true. And right now, it is a very weak voice, but there are times when it is loud and clear and I'll actually turn my ear to listen to it rather than trust in the truth."

"You need to remember the words your child taught you," I instructed, speaking slowly and with emphasis. "You need to remember your strength and your will. You need to remember the work it has taken for you to reach this place where you and your husband have so much to offer your child. Thank the child for everything you have learned. Spend some time with him. Then, when you are ready, open your eyes. . . ."

There was a look of peacefulness on Carmen's face

when she finally opened her eyes. The tension had gone and she seemed refreshed. I suggested that she should spend time dialoguing with the image of her baby on her own and that she should use the process to condition her body for labor. Carmen was under no illusions that image guidance would be a substitute for anesthesia, but she did know that it would help her stay centered during the days before her child's arrival and possibly during labor itself.

*   *   *

Reggie was embarrassed about his problem. Years of chronic constipation had resulted in rectal surgery which had left him "impaired": in order to remove a fissure which had formed, surgeons cut through the sphincter, leaving him with limited bowel control. The only way he could function in the work world was to establish a regular schedule, so that he could time his comings and goings around when he needed to use the bathroom. Any change in schedule—an early morning meeting or a trip out of town—left him in fear of a possible accident. As his job began to require more and more flexibility, so Reggie's anxiety level began to build. He seriously considered whether he should look for a new position.

"I think if I could just go back and see where this pattern of constipation began, I might be able to get over it," he explained.

"Is this something you feel ready to do?"

"Yes, I have some hunches as to what happened, but I do feel uncomfortable talking about them. This isn't the nicest of topics."

"That's O.K. The important thing is to get you functioning again. Why don't we begin with some relaxation work and go from there . . . ?"

Because of his embarrassment, I spent longer than usual

leading him though breathing exercises; I encouraged him to invite a friend on the journey (in his imagination, that is) so that he wouldn't feel quite so threatened. My main concern was to establish a "safe environment." I instructed him to return to some point in his childhood where going to the bathroom became an issue.

"I can see myself sitting on the toilet in my aunt's house," he said. "I'm about five years old—chubby, red in the face from pushing—and my shorts are hanging around my sneakers. The door is closed, but not locked and I'm afraid someone will come in."

"Why are you afraid, Reggie?"

"It's my aunt—she won't allow me to lock the door because she's got several children in foster care whom she's trying to potty train. I stay with her after morning kindergarten each day until my mom has finished work."

"What does your aunt do?"

"Well, first she'll starting hollering and banging on the door, and then she'll burst into the room, and make me get off."

"I know this will be unpleasant, but I would like you to remember a specific time when this happened."

"O.K. Again, I'm about five or six and I'm sitting on the john. I'm having a hard time going because I held it all day. Suddenly, there's the screaming and banging on the door, and my aunt barges in. Aunt Lydia—I hated her. She is holding a baby on one hip and is dragging a toddler by the arm. Both are sniveling. She tells me to get off and that I've been in the bathroom long enough. I tell her that I'm not finished and she says that's too bad because there's only one bathroom in the house and she needs it. . . ."

"What happens?"

"Well, I'm terrified of Aunt Lydia so I do as she says. I

still haven't gone and my tummy hurts, but I get off anyway. I'm embarrassed at her seeing me with my pants down. I feel like dirt. . . ."

"Let's try this scene again," I directed. "Imagine yourself back on the toilet, trying to go; Aunt Lydia is outside the door, banging away and yelling. I'll be Aunt Lydia and you be five year old Reggie. Let's see if we can change the script."

I knocked on a nearby table to make it sound as though someone was at the door.

"Who's there?" asked Reggie.

"Aunt Lydia," I said. "I need the bathroom, so hurry up and finish what you're doing."

"I can't," said Reggie. "I need a little more time."

"I said get out of there. Didn't you hear me?"

"Yes, but I need to finish first. Please stop banging and shouting and I'll be out in a minute—I'm almost ready."

"All right, but don't be long. I want to put the baby on the toilet."

I waited a few seconds, then spoke in my usual voice.

"Well, how do you feel now?"

"Much better," said Reggie. "I felt as though I was really putting dear Aunt Lydia in her place. It was good to be able to stand up to her."

"Focus on the image of yourself, sitting on the toilet, with Aunt Lydia locked outside the bathroom door. Tell yourself, out loud, over and over again, 'I have a right to my privacy.' Then, when you're ready, open your eyes."

As we processed what had happened, both of us knew that it would take time to know whether or not the problem of constipation would disappear. I suggested that Reggie should go back to the bathroom scene in his own imagination, and should practice asking Aunt Lydia to leave. We would meet again in a month to see if there had been any change in his health.

*   *   *

Jon was a returned volunteer from Nicaragua who came to me with severe back pain. His time in central America had been cut short by a car accident, and he returned to Chicago for rest and healing. Though he had been back for several months and though he had consulted a variety of specialists, the pain did not ease. Someone suggested using imagery for relief; my name surfaced as a possible resource. The image he brought with him was that of a bent stick with holes in it.

"How did the stick get bent, Jon?" I asked.

"From the weather, from time, from trying to stay strong. The wind bent it and people picked it up and threw it away. At first they had tried to burn it, but it was too strong because of the tree it came from and the wood it was made of."

"Can you describe the tree?"

"It was large—so large that people could sit under it and enjoy its shade. The branch was one branch of many. . . ."

"Does the branch feel unique in any way?"

"Yes, it's shaped differently. Sticks wear down but this one keeps going. It's strong because of the influence of the big tree."

"How did the stick get holes in it?"

"When it fell and even before then—when it was swaying up in the tree, among the other branches. Parts of it wore down."

"It sounds as though the stick has been used a lot."

"Not really—it has been a part of, it has worked with others."

"What does the stick think about the way it looks?"

"It likes the way it was when it was new and strong on the tree, but it knows the shape it has now is the shape God meant it to be."

"Does the stick believe God wants it to be unique, to be bent with holes?" I asked, beginning to sense that something in Jon made him want to cling to his injury.

"Yeah, it's also unique because it survives and keeps on going. People see it as interesting."

"Ask the stick if it would like to be straight and have the holes filled in."

"Maybe," said Jon with evident hesitation.

"If the stick could imagine itself differently, how would it look?"

"It would be part of a trunk that's strong and holds many branches together; it would only fall when the whole tree dies. It would like to be part of a tree in the middle of a forest."

"What kind of a tree would the stick like to be a part of?"

"A tree that can stand among other trees—a tree that can see mountains and oceans. People see it and think how big and great it is."

"Is there anything else about the tree?"

"Its beauty. It flowers at different times of year. There are animals running around it."

"Ask the tree if it has any wisdom to share with you at this time," I instructed, feeling that we had not got very far with this initial dialogue.

"It says that to grow needs time, space and patience. Sometimes it grew five feet in a year. Other years, it didn't grow at all. It's stupid to be impatient."

"Does the tree think that the stick needs patience?"

"The stick needs it but has it. It is still in one piece—not broken into little pieces."

"Ask the tree how long the stick is going to hurt."

"As long as it exists."

"What does the tree mean by this?" Again, I felt that something in Jon was clutching at pain.

"The stick will travel right—it may be in ruins or thrown around and sometimes it will hurt to move, but the stick will see new places."

"Ask the tree if the stick has anything to learn from its pain."

"I hear 'wisdom,' 'survival,' 'integrity,' 'perseverance,' " said Jon, concentrating on each word as he repeated what he heard.

"Tell the tree that sometimes the stick hurts too much and see what the tree tells you."

"It says this is O.K., to be patient, and not to let the hurt control me."

"Ask the tree how you can stop letting the hurt control you."

"It says I should share it with others, and that I need to admit that it's there."

"Ask the tree if there's other pain which you have not yet acknowledged."

"There probably is, but it's hard to ask the tree this because the tree let the stick go."

"Ask the tree why it let the stick go."

"Because there's no control. It was time. Sometimes, life has to go on and things get let go."

"Did you want to leave?"

"In time, but not at that moment. I wasn't secure yet. I needed the nutrients and the support."

"What does the tree mean to you?"

"Mother, strength, home, beginning place. . . ."

"When you left home, was it time? Did you want to leave?"

"Yeah."

"Have you been able to return home at all?"

"For a weekend."

"Is home a happy place for you?"

"Sometimes it's chaotic; sometimes it's happy; sometimes it's difficult. When I'm there, it's hard. . . ."

"Ask the stick what it would like to do."

"It dreams of becoming a part of something, a mantle, a piece of a rocking chair. It would hurt less to be part of something."

"Where is life in the stick? Where does it find its strength?"

"From its uniqueness, its shape, its material."

"Imagine the stick without holes and not bent. How would it feel?"

"It would feel awkward. It doesn't know how to be without defects."

"Imagine the stick, in all its defects, waiting in a forest. Does it want to be healed?"

"It would like to be stronger."

"What is stopping the stick from being whole?"

"People."

"Which people?"

"Just others who say the stick is bent."

"So because people say the stick is bent, it stays bent?"

"Yes."

"Suppose people told the stick to stop being bent, would it stay bent?"

"It would feel confused and relieved."

"Why?"

"Because it can feel straight again but because it can also see that others are weak."

"What changes are needed?"

"It needs to feel strength—it has this already but

doesn't realize this. It needs to be happy where it is, to enjoy life, to take challenges as they come, but to see them as an adventure. . . ."

"Is the stick willing to make these changes?"

"Yes, but it will be hard. Change is difficult."

"What is the stick most afraid of?"

"Not being able to be part of something, of losing faith."

"What does the stick mean by losing its faith?"

"Sometimes, if it's running around and feels as though it is in control, it doesn't feel as though it needs faith in God."

"But when the stick is hurting, it can turn to God?"

"Yes. It's easier to be in relationship with God when I am hurting because God is always present as a healer."

"Imagine yourself looking at God. What does God say?"

" 'I believe in you, I'll heal you, I love you, I'll care for you, I don't want you to be hurt.' "

"Do you believe God?"

"Yes and no. I don't believe he doesn't want me to hurt. I've seen so much suffering—mothers suffering . . . children dying in my yard in Nicaragua . . . kids sick . . . people fighting. . . . I've seen pain. I believe God wants pain to be a part of my life."

"Ask God how much God wants you to suffer."

"Enough that I feel part of the others, but then I'm to take that pain and be strong enough to stop it."

"Ask God what God wants you to do once you are healed."

"God wants me to speak out for justice, to be available to people, to smile so others might smile, and to cry when I need to cry."

"Is this what you want for yourself?"

"Yes."

"What is getting in the way of your having this?"

"Those who don't give me the chance, not having enough confidence. . . ."

"Why don't you have confidence?"

"I don't know."

"Ask God."

"Because I want too much for myself. When I was young, I always tried to compete, was never affirmed."

"Ask God how you can gain more confidence."

"By being happy with who I am. By exercising, by taking care of my other needs, by taking each day one at a time."

"Is there anything else you want to ask God?"

"I ask if there is anyone special to be with me when I am down in the future—I hear, 'in time.' "

"What must you do until then?"

"Talk to the friends I have now . . . pray . . . spend time with children because they're the ones who provide happiness. . . ."

"Do you feel ready to ask God for healing?"

"Yes—I've started to."

"Jon, your back will find healing when you desire to be healed. Focus on the presence of God. Feel this presence surrounding you and filling you. . . . Now focus on the bent stick and its holes. Know that what makes the stick unique is God alone; the stick does not have to continue suffering to be pleasing to God. Know that you will be able to serve God the most fully when you allow God to heal you. . . ."

In many ways, the dialogue I have recorded seems repetitive and somewhat tedious. On the printed page, it is difficult to see that it is going anywhere, and yet, as I worked with Jon, I had a strong intuitive hunch that he himself was the primary reason he had not found relief from his back pain. The "break" for me came when he began speaking about the suffering he had witnessed in Nicaragua; I realized that he felt he did not deserve relief from his pain. His attitude was, "If others have to suffer so much, what right do I have to be healed?" As we processed our session, I asked him to consider how much more useful he would be to God in promoting justice if he were pain-free. I also suggested that he should examine some of his childhood issues, particularly in terms of his never having been affirmed. His anger with the tree for letting him go was there under the surface, as, I suspected, was his rage with his parents. The back injury had been real, but it was spiritual and emotional issues that were presently getting in the way of full recovery.

Future Possibilities
for Image Guidance

Initially, I had thought of grouping my final comments under the not very original heading of "Concluding Thoughts." It did not take me very long, however, to remember that *Image Guidance: A Tool for Spiritual Direction* was still in press when many new applications surfaced. On the one hand, I had wanted to delay publication to include these new applications; on the other, I was anxious to see my groundwork in print as soon as possible. And so it was that the book came to birth when much of my work was still in its infancy.

Looking back, I still believe this was the right decision. Having a book "out" gave me opportunities to take image guidance into the public arena. Invitations for workshops surfaced, as did opportunities for working with private clients. It was also during this time that I became affiliated with Psychological Resources, a downtown Chicago practice with a new suite of southside offices, conveniently close to my home. With the generous support of Drs. Dan and Kathleen O'Grady and their colleagues, I used this space to meet with individual clients and to hold workshops on topics ranging from dream interpretation to healing the inner child. None of this would have happened without the publication of the book.

Looking forward, I see that my main focus with image guidance will continue to lie in the spiritual realm. It is no accident that many of the clients who come my way have spiritual issues, in addition to physical and emotional issues. I do not set out to impose my own belief system and symbology on my clients; rather, I allow their images to arise spontaneously, taking them from where they "are" to where they need to go. I simply follow the lead of whatever images surface and, more often than not, these images are "religious" in nature or lead to religious insights. I have come to believe that people very often find exactly the kind of "helpers" that they need for a particular stage of their journey and that this is why my own skills as a spiritual director come into play, even when I am working on health issues.

One arena in which I have had very little experience is mental health, but I do believe that just as physiological ailments can be spiritual in origin, so, too, can mental afflictions. This became apparent in one case where I was called in to be a consultant. Since the client in question was "borderline psychotic," I agreed to meet with her in the presence of her psychologist, so that there was no confusion as to whose patient she really was and so that there could be the necessary intervention, if a difficult situation should arise. For four years, the client had been obsessed with vampire possession; believing that someone had imposed a voodoo curse on her, she had gradually lost touch with reality, moving more and more deeply into a terrifying landscape of hideous creatures who teased and tormented her, lusted after her and relentlessly pursued her. She was so terrified by these apparitions that she moved back in with her parents, refused to leave the house without them, and began to degenerate physically. Since conventional therapy had had limited success, her psychologist wondered whether image guidance could be of use. I had some concerns about using the process with somebody as seemingly unstable as Tanya, but since the psychologist would be present and since the client was in a desperate situation, I decided to take the risk.

We had barely gotten into introductions when Tanya began to see one of the vampires who had oppressed her so vividly. I had no plan of action when we met, but my pastoral instincts told me to combine image guidance with some of the principles of exorcism as I understood them. I calmed Tanya by instructing her to hold the cross she was wearing round her neck, and lit a candle that was conveniently at hand. Then, I told her to close her eyes and to see herself protected by a white light—God's light—and to know that she was protected from anything harmful. She described the vampire as she saw it, trembling as she did so; she was obviously gripped by fear. Reminding her that she was protected by God's light, I instructed her to ask the vampire its name; when she had learned that it was "Franceso," I told her to inform it that it had no power over her, that, with God's strength, she was stronger than it was, and that from now on, it could do nothing to harm her. Finally, when it was evident that Tanya was convinced of the truth of these words, I asked her to command the vampire to leave her in the name of Jesus Christ. This she did, with obvious relief. We concluded by praying the Lord's Prayer together. Before she left, she asked me to write down what she was to say to the vampire should it return; she repeated these words to herself several times, fully believing that she could cast out any evil spirits at will. According to her psychologist, she has remembered these words and has regained much of her former independence. The whole experience was, for me, a lesson in the power of religious symbolism, dramatic effects, prayer and the imagination in healing the psyche.

There are a number of uses for image guidance with which I have not yet experimented. For example, I could see image guidance being used in nursing homes and hospices to prepare the aged or terminally ill to die peacefully. By imaging an afterlife, by making peace with one's past, by accepting one's mortality, the dying could "let go" and "move on." This is work for which chaplains and hospice workers could be trained. I could also see image guidance being used in pediatrics: children could learn to see their illnesses or disabilities as parts of themselves (if the conditions are irreversible) or as enemies to be overcome (if the child's energy is needed to ward off invasive bacteria, etc.). Using image guidance as a diagnostic tool both with children and with adults is another possible application: through imagery, one can pinpoint symptoms and even receive "feedback" from the images themselves about what is going on and about what needs to be done. Group image guidance—as for example, with cancer patients or with diabetics—could be yet another development. Here, as in the previous examples, specialists would be the most appropriate image guidance counselors; another possibility would be for "lay" image guidance counselors to be assisted by health care experts who could suggest strategies, direct imagery and interpret the data.

I close as I began—with the humble recognition that image guidance is much bigger than I am and that it has possibilities which lie far beyond either my imagination or my abilities. I hope that others will take this gift of the imagination into those places where, for very good reasons, I fear to tread. . . .

A Screening Tool To Use with Potential Image Guidance Clients

Since image guidance is a powerful way of accessing the unconscious and since material from all of one's life can surface unexpectedly during the process, it is highly important that the guide should be familiar with your medical and psychological history. Please be honest in your responses, so that the guide can decide whether or not this would be an appropriate intervention.

NAME:
DATE OF BIRTH:
ADDRESS:

TELEPHONE: (HM)   (WK)

HEALTH CAREGIVERS:
TITLE AND NAME: TELEPHONE:
ROLE:

TITLE AND NAME: TELEPHONE:
ROLE:

TITLE AND NAME: TELEPHONE:
ROLE:

1. What makes you seek out image guidance at this time?

2. What are your expectations of the process?

3. Have you ever worked with imagery before? If so, with what results?

4. Have you discussed image guidance with your health caregivers? If so, what were their reactions?

5. Are you presently in therapy? If so, have you discussed image guidance with your psychologist/psychiatrist/social worker? Does he/she approve of this process?

6. Do you have a history of depression? If so, have you ever been hospitalized for depression? Have you ever been on medication for depression? How recently have you been treated for depression? If you have been treated for depression during the last year, please give the name, address and phone number of the doctor who treated you or who is currently treating you.

7. Did you experience any childhood traumas which still cause you pain?

8. Did you experience any childhood traumas which you have consciously blocked from your memory or which you suspect you may have experienced but aren't quite sure?

9. Have you experienced any traumas in adult life which still evoke pain or fear?

10. Is there any other information which could help your guide decide whether image guidance would be a safe and effective intervention for you?